Handbook of Academic Writing
for Librarians

Christopher V. Hollister

Association of College and Research Libraries
A division of the American Library Association
Chicago, 2013

The paper used in this publication meets the minimum requirements of American National Standard for Information Sciences–Permanence of Paper for Printed Library Materials, ANSI Z39.48-1992. ∞

Library of Congress Cataloging-in-Publication Data

Hollister, Christopher Vance.
  Handbook of academic writing for librarians / Christopher V. Hollister.
     pages cm
  Includes bibliographical references and index.
  ISBN 978-0-8389-8648-6 (pbk. : alk. paper) 1. Library science—Authorship-
-Handbooks, manuals, etc. 2. Information science—Authorship—Handbooks,
manuals, etc. 3. Library science literature—Publishing—Handbooks, manuals,
etc. 4. Information science literature—Publishing—Handbooks, manuals, etc.
5. Academic writing—Handbooks, manuals, etc. I. Title.
  Z669.7.H65 2013
  808.06'602

2013016864

Printed in the United States of America.

14 13 12 11 10   5 4 3 2 1

Table of Contents

Acknowledgements

Any acknowledgements relative to this *Handbook of Academic Writing for Librarians* must begin with Kathryn Deiss, Content Strategist for ACRL. It is difficult to describe Kathryn's importance to this work without bestowing lavish praises. Hopefully it will suffice to assert the following for the record: Kathryn is primarily responsible for the idea of this book being realized, and she is equally responsible for me feeling at home as an ACRL author. Thanks, Kathryn!

Grateful acknowledgement is given to my many friends and colleagues in the University at Buffalo Libraries for their generous support and countless instances of kindness throughout the year that was required to write this book. In particular, I wish to thank the Head of Public Services, Margaret Wells, and the Vice Provost for the University Libraries, H. Austin Booth, for their continued and enthusiastic support. Readers should know that Ms. Wells and Ms. Booth were instrumental in my being granted a six month sabbatical, without which the completion this handbook would be in doubt.

Grateful acknowledgement is also given to the many LIS educators, journal editors, manuscript reviewers, practitioners, and researchers who were generous enough to oblige my solicitations and share their expertise and opinion relative to this work; their contributions helped to inform the overall development of the text. Special thanks are given to my longtime professional confidantes, Lisa Hinchliffe and Megan Oakleaf, for their particular expert contributions.

I thank Stewart Brower, who is my dear friend and co-editor with the journal, *Communications in Information Literacy* (CIL); he was courageous enough to read through the first draft of this text and to provide the necessary criticisms. Stewart is an ongoing source of encouragement, reassurance, and perhaps most importantly, good humor. The same traits can also be attributed to my new friend and co-editor with CIL, Robert Schroeder, who, as an added benefit, inspires a renewed enthusiasm for the professional literature.

Numerous other friends and colleagues have contributed to this work in ways that they likely do not recognize. I thank the following individuals, who are abundantly supportive in their own unique and meaningful ways: Frank Ratel, Tom Rogers, Tim Galvin, Scott Hollander, Adrian (AJ) Johnson, Lauren Johnson, Chris Parker, Dave Friedrich, George Smith, and Gerry Rising.

The concluding and most affectionate acknowledgements are reserved for my wife, Theresa, and my three daughters, Jessica, Kayla, and Sydney. I feel blessed each and every day.

Christopher V. Hollister
February, 2013

Preface

The *Handbook of Academic Writing for Librarians* was developed with the intention that it will serve primarily as a reference tool for the community of library and information science (LIS) professionals who are either required or encouraged to publish in the professional literature, or who simply desire to do so. This handbook was also developed for the audience of LIS students who have curricular requirements to write academic papers, or who intend to pursue careers in librarianship that may involve varying forms of professional writing. The main purposes of this text are to assist both experienced and inexperienced LIS authors in the following areas:

- The spawning and development of academic writing ideas;
- The improvement of academic writing skills;
- The contribution of useful and noteworthy ideas to the professional literature;
- The pursuit of personally and professionally fulfilling writing opportunities;
- The informed identification of suitable publishing outlets;
- The understanding and appreciation of both fundamental and evolving concepts in scholarly communication.

While developing this handbook, the author interviewed and consulted with a diverse group of widely published and highly respected LIS leaders, including educators, journal editors, manuscript reviewers, practitioners, and researchers. The goal of these conversations was to assess the perceived state of the professional literature, and to identify the particular strengths and weaknesses that are common to the community of LIS authors. There were striking similarities in the views expressed by all participants, particularly with respect to the substandard quality of writing they recognize in most forms of LIS professional writing. As a result of these conversations and the author's own experiences as a journal editor and manuscript reviewer, the present text was organized into six broad chapters: 1. Elements of Good Academic Writing, 2. Elements of Writing Well, 3. Elements of the Scholarly Paper, 4. Elements of Selecting the Right Journal, 5. Elements of the Publishing Process, and 6. Elements of the Scholarly Book. Each of these chapters is fully fleshed out in a manner that guides readers from start to finish through different concepts and stages of the writing process, but with particular emphasis and instruction on the weaknesses identified by the author and the greater community of LIS leaders.

Chapter 1: Elements of Good Academic Writing. This short, introductory chapter begins with a discussion of the specific elements that constitute good academic writing: clear thinking, hard work, and refined writing skills. The various motivations that LIS professionals may have for contributing to the literature are presented, and readers are encouraged to regard authorship as a unique and critically important opportunity to contribute to professional discourse in a genuinely meaningful way. Readers are guided through the common myths of academic writing, and they are prompted to explore potentially noteworthy writing ideas in their daily professional lives.

Chapter 2: Elements of Writing Well. The greater body of this chapter is devoted to the specifics of improving one's academic writing skills in terms of structure, content, style, and mechanics. The section on writing mechanics is further subdivided into the elements of English language usage that are most commonly cited as problematic for LIS authors, with particular emphasis on the rules of grammar. Based on the aforementioned input from LIS leaders, necessary attention is also given to other writing mechanics: punctuation, spelling, capitalization, and abbreviation. Readers will find that useful examples are provided for each area that is covered.

Chapter 3: Elements of the Scholarly Paper. This chapter begins with a definition and a brief history of the scholarly paper; the intent is to impress upon readers the long and meaningful traditions inherent to constructing disciplinary arguments by way of the scholarly paper. The greater body of this chapter, however, is devoted to the essential parts of the scholarly paper:

abstract, introduction, literature review, method, results, discussion, and conclusions. All these parts are fully delineated and include useful examples that are harvested from the literature. Equal emphasis is given to both the essential functions of each part of the scholarly paper, and to how those parts fit together to form effective arguments. Readers are also instructed on the subtle and significant differences that exist between scholarly LIS papers and those that are published in the other social sciences.

Chapter 4: Elements of Selecting the Right Journal. This chapter begins with instruction on finding appropriate LIS journals for one's scholarly work with baseline qualifying criteria: subject matter, intended audience, types of journals, and types of articles. Most of this chapter, however, is devoted to selecting the right LIS journals based on a more sophisticated calculus that includes analyses and even criticisms of common bibliometric tools and professional perceptions of journal prestige. Readers are encouraged to think critically about traditional journal ranking methods when selecting publishers for their work; they are also encouraged to fully investigate potential journal publishers, and to rely more heavily on their professional philosophies for decision-making. Additionally, this chapter includes germane discussions of open access, copyright, and even the particulars of querying journal editors.

Chapter 5: Elements of the Publishing Process. This chapter begins with practical advice for preparing one's manuscript for submission, and also for the submission process itself. A greater share of the chapter, however, is devoted to lesser understood matters of the publication process such as peer review and editorial decisions. Readers are led step-by-step through the publication process, beginning from manuscript submission, through internal journal operations, and ultimately to the issuing of editorial decisions. The roles of editors and reviewers are illuminated, and the process of peer review is clarified with fair, but necessary criticisms. Readers are also provided with examples of different editorial decisions, the likely reasons behind those decisions, and recommendations for how they should respond.

Chapter 6: Elements of the Scholarly Book. This chapter is devoted entirely to the distinctive undertaking of writing and publishing the scholarly book. As the chapter begins, readers are guided through the necessary processes of vetting, selecting, and querying book publishers; the basic similarities of working with journal publishers are shown, but the unique aspects of working with book publishers are accentuated. A significant portion of the chapter is devoted to the development of the successful book proposal. Readers are also instructed on the essential, but evolving elements of contemporary book contacts that must be considered, and in many instances negotiated. Finally, readers are provided with a checklist of practical recommendations and effective strategies for successfully completing book-length writing projects and edited volumes.

Content, Narration, and Style

The overriding purpose of this book is to assist LIS professionals and students with becoming better academic writers; to that end, the author's goal is to lead first by example, creating a reference work that is practical and fresh, and genuinely readable. The intent is to present this handbook in a manner that is instructional, but not didactic, and enjoyable, but not trite. Readers will note particular characteristics of content, narration, and style that are uncharacteristic of previous academic LIS writing guides. To begin, this handbook is focused on scholarly writing; it does not include advice, recommendations, or strategies for authors of popular, trade, or other non-academic work. This handbook is not intended as a replacement for comprehensive publishing guides, multidisciplinary manuals of style, or authoritative English usage texts. Instead, it is intended as a complementary reference tool for an audience of LIS scholars, and it is targeted to that audience's unique writing and publishing needs.

Readers will note that this handbook is presented in the formal, third-person narrative style; this is done primarily to exemplify the predominant and preferred manner of scholarly writing. The intent is also to demonstrate that the effective use of scholarly writing can be a compelling, and even an elegant form of argument, discourse, and presentation. Readers will also note the abundance of supporting, cited evidence throughout the course of this text; this is likewise included to exemplify sound scholarly writing practices, but with the added benefit of underscoring essential ideas.

Readers will find instances throughout the course of this handbook in which different sections overlap, and where relative ideas are necessarily repeated. It is the author's assertion that no elements of the writing process are mutually exclusive, and that important points should be reiterated for emphasis. Finally, readers will likely note an unmistakable flavor of opinion in some of the subject matter presented in this text. By virtue of the author's aforementioned consultations with LIS educators, journal editors, manuscript reviewers, practitioners, and researchers, it can be steadfastly asserted that any opinions expressed in this text are widely shared by leaders in the LIS community. Furthermore, the publisher of this text strongly encouraged the inclusion of evocative, but informed and opinion-driven content.

Form and Function

The maxim "form follows function" serves as an overriding philosophy of this handbook. Although this philosophy is more commonly associated with the field of creative writing, it also holds true for scholarly writing, and that assertion is elucidated and reiterated throughout the course of the text: The form of one's writing should follow its essential function. As readers will recognize, this same philosophical trajectory is also applied to fundamental elements of the writing process that originate with one's scholarly ideas and motivations. That is, the development of one's ideas should precede and inform the purpose for communicating them in writing: not vice versa. Furthermore, the practical considerations for communicating one's ideas should drive the decision regarding suitable format (i.e., book, journal article, weblog), which in turn, should lead to the selection of an appropriate medium or a publisher, and so on.

To summarize, the functions of academic writing and its many processes should always precede, and thus determine the form of that which follows. Any disruptions or unnatural impositions relative to this continuum can and generally do have an adverse effect on the overall quality, reach, and impact of one's written work. The author of this handbook is a fervent believer in this philosophy.

1
Elements of Good Academic Writing

Introduction

Good academic writing is not a mystery; it is a product of clear thinking, hard work, and refined writing skills. The clear thinking part involves more than one's knowledge or expertise in a subject area. Authors must see, understand, and be able to articulate how their work relates to the works of others in the field, how it fits within the framework of contemporary theory, and how it contributes to an ongoing discourse within their particular area of practice or study. The hard work part is straightforward; writing is a discipline that requires the same amount of effort that one devotes to the actual subject matter of their work. The refined writing skills part includes more than the mastery of grammar, vocabulary, and overall usage. Good writing requires authors to master forms of expression, and most importantly, to develop their own personal style. The purpose of this chapter is to assist library and information science (LIS) professionals with all these elements of academic writing. The information to follow is primarily intended for authors of scholarly papers (i.e., journal articles), but most of the material can also be applied to books, book chapters, scholarly weblogs, and other forms of academic writing.

Academic Writing Motivations

For many LIS professionals—particularly faculty librarians and library educators—the impetus for writing is related to requirements for appointment, promotion, and tenure. It is disingenuous to deny this as a primary motivator. As with other disciplines, this manner of incentive feeds into an ever-hungry and self-fulfilling publishing enterprise, and ultimately it has an impact on both the strengths and the weaknesses of the professional literature. Certainly, there are other motivations for writing that apply, which are predictable and very human. However, the most meaningful reason behind any form of academic writing is that an author wishes to participate in professional discourse, and that he or she has something important and unique to contribute. As difficult as it may be at times, authors are encouraged to focus on this as their primary motivation. Otherwise the writing process will be less fulfilling, and resulting written works will be less compelling.

Academic Writing Myths

Myth: Nothing to Contribute. Myth number one among an unknown, but very real percentage of LIS professionals is that they have little or nothing important to contribute. On the contrary, all librarians, regardless of their specialty, have a community of peers that share the same professional challenges and potential solutions. Systems librarians labor to develop innovative open source software solutions; school media librarians collaborate with English language arts teachers to bolster student reading skills; directors use survey data to demonstrate the value of their libraries; and instruction librarians apply principles derived from contemporary learning theory to improve their teaching skills. These are examples of shared experiences, and the unique manners by which LIS professionals create, develop, implement, and assess improvements and solutions are, by definition, contributions to the profession. Professional contributions may be practical, research-based, or theoretical, or they may be successes or failures, but for the betterment of LIS, they should be shared. The primary mechanism for sharing new disciplinary ideas is evolving in terms of format and dissemination, but it continues to be the professional literature.

Myth: Not Worthy. Myth number two among some LIS professionals is that their contributions are unworthy of inclusion in the academic branch of the literature. For these professionals there exists an atmosphere of mystique about academic literature. This is particularly true with respect to peer-reviewed journals. However, the myth is easily debunked, and the mystique is easily dissipated. As the term "peer-reviewed" suggests, manuscript reviewers are peers in one's field. Reviewers for *Journal of Access Services* are access services librarians; reviewers for *Communications in Information Literacy* are instruction librarians; and reviewers for *Journal of the Medical Library Association* are health sciences librarians. As peers, these individuals share the same challenges and experiences, they understand the unique nature of their area in the profession, and they value new contributions. Not to be forgotten, journal editors are likewise peers in the profession. The keys to successfully publishing in scholarly journals or in any other academic venues are as follows: proper motivation, unique subject matter, good writing skills, and matching one's work to suitable publishers or publications. These core elements of academic writing are delineated throughout the course of this text.

1.1 Getting Started

Generating Ideas

The greater body of scholarly LIS literature is a product of ideas that were generated by practitioners and researchers for the purpose of improving practice and advancing the discipline. One can imagine endless examples of this from the daily job responsibilities of all types of LIS professionals: a cataloger may develop an innovative protocol for metadata quality control; a consortium of hospital librarians may implement a more efficient system of interlibrary lending; a public library director may institute controversial rules for collecting young adult literature; or a library educator may study the prevalence of library anxiety among first-year college students. These experiments, innovations, and implementations are intended to improve professional practice in the microcosm of individual departments, institutions, or networks. However, because they relate to experiences that are shared by peers in the greater community of LIS professionals, these examples also have the potential to advance the practice and the discipline of library and information science on a larger scale. This is done primarily by way of professional discourse in the scholarly literature.

Most LIS professionals have experience with creating, implementing, researching, and even assessing initiatives, programs, and services for the betterment of practice at their own institutions. Therefore, most LIS professionals have the potential subject material for writing an academic paper or book. Published works are often the end result of a multistep process that begins with developing an improvement or a solution, assessing its effectiveness, and then reporting on it. Findings are typically reported first to unit heads, directors, deans, or chairpersons. If the initiative, program, or service has positive outcomes, the responsible practitioner may volunteer, or may be asked to present on his or her accomplishment or findings to other departments or groups. If there are implications or applicable lessons for LIS professionals at other institutions, the responsible practitioner may submit proposals to present at regional or even national conferences. As a natural next step, the professional presentation is often reworked into the form of a scholarly paper or book.

As noted, LIS professionals commonly report on and write about their successes. However, their failures can be equally useful and instructive. For practitioners, new or modified initiatives do not always work as planned. For researchers, study results do not always support hypotheses. Experimentation and failure are natural components of LIS practice and research, and they are essential for continued growth. Although LIS literature does not include an abundance of failed experiments, authors are encouraged to also consider this type of information as potential subject matter for their writing.

Importance of Being Noteworthy

In order for an author's work to be publishable, it needs to be thoroughly researched, professionally presented, and well written; these elements are obvious, and they are delineated throughout the course of this text. The element of the scholarly paper or book that authors should consider before they begin writing is the noteworthiness of the subject matter. There is little value in writing a paper or a book that lacks new information. Insufficiently unique works are unlikely to survive review or editorial processes because they add nothing new to the practice or the discipline, and therefore, they do not qualify as contributions to the literature. The subject matter of a paper or book can be unique in the following ways:

> **New Methods or Theory.** In this type of paper or book, authors present new methods of professional practice or research, or they propose new theory related to practice or research. This type of scholarly work has the potential to be the most impactful, because it represents new thinking in the discipline, and potentially, new directions. For the same reasons, this type of work also has the potential to be the most controversial. Authors of these papers or books have an exceptionally high level of expertise in the relative subject matter argued or presented.

New Evidence for Previous Methods or Theory. In this type of paper or book, authors present new evidence in support of previous methods of professional practice, or in support of previous theory related to practice or research. This is a common type of scholarly work published in LIS literature. Most case study papers, for instance, present evidence in support of established methods or theories. Similarly, most research papers in LIS make use of established social science methodologies and relative theories. Authors are cautioned, however, that such works may not be regarded as having sufficiently unique information to qualify for publication. This type of scholarship must include explicitly new implications in terms of ongoing developments in the discipline.

Previous Methods or Theory in a New Way. In this type of paper or book, authors propose new interpretations of previous practice, research, or theory, and the relative implications for professional practice. Generally this is done by connecting two or more previously unrelated works. An author may, for example, demonstrate the parallels between a case study paper on the use of web communication tools to improve student engagement and a theoretical paper that proposes connectivism as a new learning theory, and then propose the implications in terms of credit-bearing information literacy courses. Albeit this is an uncommon type of scholarly work in LIS literature, it has the potential to be particularly impactful.

Determining Noteworthiness. It is a significant challenge for even the most informed LIS authors to consistently know if their writing ideas qualify as unique contributions. Authors should always begin their investigation of this by conducting a review of the professional literature. Fortunately, this type of research is one of the LIS professional's fortes, and here, it serves several relevant and highly useful purposes. Beyond validating the unique nature of one's ideas, this type of research reveals gaps in the literature that need to be filled, it shows authors how their ideas relate to those of others in the field, and it helps them to form and organize arguments for the importance of their own work. Ultimately, these are the points that authors must assert in the discussion and conclusion sections of their writing projects. Researching the professional literature is also the first step to organizing and preparing the literature review part of a scholarly paper, and it can help authors to identify potentially suitable journals. To be thorough, authors are also encouraged to consult the literature of related disciplines, monitor professional discussion lists and weblogs, review presentation abstracts from professional conferences, and conduct advanced-level searches on the free web.

From Ideas to Writing

Once an author has determined the unique nature of a writing idea and identified the need for it by way of a gap or a weakness in the literature, he or she should begin crafting the first draft of a highly condensed overview. If an author intends to write an article, this will qualify as the abstract, and if an author is considering a book, this will be the heart of the proposal. The condensed overview serves many worthwhile purposes: it helps the author to focus on and refine his or her approach to the main topic or argument; it provides the initial direction, organization, and skeletal structure of the intended work; it serves as point of return to keep the author on track; and it functions as the selling point for prospective editors and publishers. The fundamentals of crafting effective abstracts and proposals are detailed respectively in the Elements of the Scholarly Paper and Elements of the Scholarly Book sections of this text.

2

Elements of Writing Well

This chapter is devoted to specific ways that LIS authors can refine their academic writing skills; it is organized into four subsections: content, structure, style, and mechanics. Information included here does not replace the authoritative, comprehensive writing style manuals that all authors are strongly encouraged to keep in their preferred work spaces. Instead, this part of the text serves as a complementary, discipline-specific guide that addresses particular academic writing strengths and weaknesses of LIS authors. A group of widely published and highly respected LIS professionals was consulted for the purpose of identifying the necessary information to be included in this section of the text. These experts represent a wide variety of LIS educators, journal editors, manuscript reviewers, practitioners, and researchers.

2.1 Content

Focus

The overall focus of one's written work is paramount; it should be accessible to the reader in meaningful and relevant ways. This is accomplished by presenting the main topic in a manner that is not perceived as being too broad or too narrow for the intended audience. Whereas written works presented too broadly are perceived as uninformative, uninspiring, unoriginal, and unworthy of publication, those presented too narrowly are perceived as esoteric, inapplicable, irrelevant, and likewise not publishable. This is particularly true for journal article and book chapter manuscripts, but it is germane for book-length works as well.

Too Broad. In an effort to avoid their work being perceived as too broad, authors should assume a readership of experts in the field. It is unnecessary to devote lengthy passages to information commonly known among peers in the profession. It is, for example, unnecessary to define or describe the purpose of subject headings for an intended audience of cataloger librarians. Authors should avoid unnecessary background information, such as institutional settings or histories, user demographics, or user statistics, unless that information is absolutely pertinent to the main topic. Authors are also encouraged to avoid statements of the obvious (e.g., "An effective reference interview is necessary for helping patrons to find..."), or overreaching, unsupported discussion of theoretical frameworks (e.g., "Teacher librarians understand the shortcomings of behaviorist theory...").

Too Narrow. In an effort to avoid their work being perceived as too narrow, authors should clearly express the implications of their work in a context that is relevant and meaningful to peers in the field. When the subject matter of a written work has no bearing elsewhere, it serves no useful purpose as an addition to the literature. Beyond stating the importance of their work, authors should provide relevant and demonstrative examples (e.g., "The assessment instrument developed for this study can be modified for use in similarly sized rural public libraries..."). Authors should also avoid the assumption that readers understand all the details of the context presented in their work. For example, not all health science librarians understand the dynamics of providing information services for surgical faculty in a clinical setting; not all school media librarians understand the particular needs of gifted students; and not all LIS educators understand the challenges of international online education. The provision of these details is often what distinguishes an author's work as a unique and useful contribution.

Originality and Ownership

As noted, unique subject matter is essential for scholarly works to be considered as useful additions to LIS or any other body of disciplinary literature. However, LIS authors commonly fail to sufficiently articulate the originality of their work. Authors are encouraged to unabashedly claim their own ideas, state the significance of their work, and assert the newness of it. The conventions of academic writing provide apposite places for authors to state their claims. For instance, authors of scholarly papers can assert newness and ownership in the abstract (e.g., "In this case study the author demonstrates..."), in the literature review (e.g., "The author's methodology addresses shortcomings in previous studies..."), in the discussion (e.g., "Results of this study confirm the author's hypothesis..."), and in the conclusion (e.g., "The author's work validates..."). Conversely, authors are cautioned avoid overselling their work with gratuitous contentions of originality; LIS editors and reviewers are well-informed, and they are adept at calling attention to unfounded claims of ownership.

Informal Fallacy. Authors are cautioned against validating the originality of their ideas by fabricating circumstances or by constructing false arguments. This is commonly known as a "straw man argument" because it is constructed merely for the ease of confirming what an author wishes to assert, and because it is easily argued against. The most common imposition of such arguments come by way of broad, unsubstantiated generalizations or plainly false premises (e.g., "Librarians are disenchanted with the changed nature of reference desk work because…," or "Undergraduate students lack the information literacy skills necessary to…").

Scholarship

The quantity and quality of evidence that is presented relative to the main topic of one's work is critical. Authors must present ample and appropriate evidence for what they are arguing, asserting, or demonstrating, and they must do so in a scholarly manner. Written works that lack the necessary amount of relevant evidence, or those that are presented in an unscholarly manner are typically discounted by readers as being colloquial, elementary, obvious, or pedestrian, and as such, they are deemed as being unworthy additions to the literature. There are two types of evidence authors should include in their works: cited literature and supporting data.

Cited Literature Evidence. Cited literature evidence refers to previously published works that are relative to the main topic an author is arguing, asserting, or demonstrating; these works show the need for, the importance, and the originality of an author's own work. Such information is often given in the literature review section of a scholarly paper, or it may be interspersed as necessary throughout the course of longer works. The most common problems with cited literature evidence in LIS manuscripts are the following:

- *Insufficient Evidence:* Authors should include enough cited literature to fully demonstrate the need for that written work.
- *Unnecessary Evidence:* Authors should avoid weakening their argument by overselling it with redundant cited literature, or with that which gives unnecessary historical overviews.

- **Irrelevant Evidence:** Authors should avoid the use of cited literature that is not completely pertinent to the main point. The most common instance of using irrelevant evidence is the unnecessary inclusion of citations to well-known authors or source materials solely for the purpose of name or source recognition.
- **Dated Evidence:** Authors should include the most current evidence in support of their work. Editors and reviewers are highly informed peers in their respective fields of practice or research, and they will discount dated evidence as incomplete and unscholarly.
- **Incorrect Evidence:** Authors must be highly meticulous about the use of cited literature evidence. They must be certain to give complete and impeccably accurate citations, and to provide every necessary attribution to the works of other scholars. The most common instances of incorrect evidence include mismatched in-text and ending references, misspelled author names, incorrect bibliographic information, incorrect applications of required citation styles, mismatched citation styles, misattributed works, omitted attributions, and sadly, even among LIS professionals, plagiarized text.

Supporting Data Evidence. Supporting data evidence is that which is generated by way of the main subject matter in one's written work. In LIS literature, this is the data collected from a case study or a research project. Whether it is in support or in nonsupport of an author's original hypothesis, it is critical to include this evidence for the purpose of an effectively presented argument or case. Supporting data evidence is often given in the results section of a scholarly paper (see the Elements of the Scholarly Paper section), or it may be interspersed as necessary throughout the course of longer works.

Theory

Relating one's work to current theory—commonly referred to as providing a theoretical framework—is vital for many forms of scholarly writing. It is often necessary for authors to provide a theoretical framework in order for their work to have bearing and relevance in the discipline. This runs counter to the beliefs of many authors who view the inclusion of relative theory as being necessary only for so-called theoretical works. There is an important distinction to be made here: Whereas the authors of theoretical works use existing literature to advance, debunk, or revise a particular theory, the authors of other forms of scholarly communication use theory to give context and substance to their own work.

As the term implies, the theoretical framework is a structural construct; it shows how the main topic or argument of one's work is relative to and fits within the architecture of disciplinary discourse. The particular challenge for LIS scholars is to identify relevant theory, because, as McGrath (2002) noted, "In Library and Information Science (LIS), there is little formal theory to agree or disagree on" (p. 309). Even so, Pettigrew and McKechnie (2001) demonstrated through a content analysis of articles published in six LIS journals that one-third included discussion of applicable theory. The essential nature of this element to academic writing is not lost on LIS editors. Hernon, Smith, and Croxen (1993) showed that the problem of inadequate theory is identified by LIS journal editors as a chief concern and a notable reason for manuscript rejection. More recently, Weller (2001) confirmed these findings in the broader context of social science journal literature. Written works that lack an appropriate theoretical framework can be dismissed by editors and reviewers as baseless, irrelevant, poorly developed, structurally flawed, or simply uninteresting.

The inclusion of a theoretical framework in one's work is not as daunting as it may seem. By its very nature LIS is a multidisciplinary area of study, and its scholars commonly adapt relevant theoretical perspectives from other areas of study. Consider, for example, how instruction librarians effectively relate their work to learning theory, how reference librarians relate their work to communication theory, how catalogers relate their work to ontological theory, and how library deans and directors relate their work to organizational behavior theory. Library and information science is a relatively new discipline, and as such it requires the infusion of existing and abundant theory from other areas in order to grow. As McKechnie and Pettigrew (2002) asserted, "…the multidisciplinary expertise needed to increase and improve the use of theory from other disciplines and to aid in the development of new theory unique to LIS is already available in the community of scholars, a rich and underutilized treasure" (p. 415).

EXAMPLE: Introducing Theoretical Framework

Problem-based learning (PBL) is a teaching-learning process or method of instruction that is widely used in medical education curricula. Librarians play important roles as facilitators for PBL as well as guides for information resources. Involvement in PBL activities presents unique opportunities to incorporate library resources and instruction into the medical curriculum. This article reviews the problem-based learning method within the conceptual framework of the learning theory of constructivism. It describes how a medical librarian at a U.S. medical school used emerging technologies to facilitate PBL small group case discussions, guide students to quality information resources, and enhance the learning environment for the PBL process. (Mi, 2012)

EXAMPLE: Establishing Theoretical Framework

The philosophical and practical work of M. M. Bakhtin provides an important aid to theoretical grounding with regard to information seeking. In particular, his ideas of dialogic communication suggest a way to engage in the act of information seeking and the accompanying mediation. His work is especially important because of its phenomenological basis, which emphasizes the intentionality of communication, the connection of practice to being, and the relationship between self and other. Bakhtin's thought offers a framework for the rethinking of public services in libraries. (Budd, 2001)

2.2 *Structure*

Organization

Effective academic writing is organized in a clear, unambiguous, and easily understandable manner. Organization relates to the structural order of one's written work, and to the sequence, logical flow, and ultimate length of it. The structural order is dictated by a combination of factors: the standards and conventions of academic writing, the nature of the subject matter presented, and the requirements of publishers. A scholarly LIS paper, for example, may be organized according to standards set forth in a the current edition of the *Publication Manual of the American Psychological Association*, but the nature of the subject matter in that paper may not require the inclusion of a literature review or a results section. Furthermore, the intended journal for that paper may require that certain sections of it are combined, or that the completed manuscript is of a specified length. This is but one example of how combined factors dictate the appropriate organization of a paper.

Standard Organization. Authors are encouraged to commence writing within the framework of organization as set forth in their preferred or required disciplinary manual of style. For LIS authors, the most common standards are provided by the *Chicago Manual of Style* and the *Publication Manual of the American Psychological Association*. Individual publishers or publications will sometimes require that LIS authors abide by manuals of style that are less commonly used in the discipline, or by a style sheet that was developed specifically for that publisher or publication. These standard forms of organization apply for books, book chapters, scholarly papers, and most other forms of academic writing.

Headings and Subheadings. Most forms of academic writing require the use of headings and subheadings for the purpose organizing and highlighting ideas. As an example, the author of a scholarly paper may organize his or her work with the use of standard headings to indicate different sections: abstract, introduction, literature review, method, results, discussion, conclusion, and references. However, the nature of the subject matter in that paper may require the use of subheadings to highlight particular ideas relative to the main topic. Headings and subheadings are useful to the author for organizing their work, and they are helpful to the reader for following and understanding it. Authors are encouraged to abide by the following guidelines for using headings and subheadings:

- *Manuals of Style:* Abide by rules for headings and subheadings in the preferred or required manual of style as they pertain to font, indentation, letter case, and placement within the text.
- *Publisher Guidelines:* Abide by rules for headings and subheadings stipulated by the publisher.
- *Fragmentation:* Avoid creating unnecessary levels of subheadings; this is confusing to the reader. Consolidate levels of presented information wherever possible.
- *Concision:* Avoid any unnecessary description or other wording; lengthy headings and subheadings defeat their own purpose.
- *Function:* Allow the formation of headings and subheadings to be dictated by the nature of subject matter in the text. Place them in an order that follows the logical trajectory of an argument or presentation, or an order that mirrors their placement in other sections of a given work. Avoid the forced imposition of headings and subheadings that are arbitrary or irrelevant to the main topic.
- *Alphabetization and Numeration:* Make only limited use of letters and numbers to reflect the organization of headings and subheadings. Multiple levels of subheadings with letters and numbers are confusing to readers; they give the impression that one's work is merely the presentation of lists.

Logical Flow. The organization of a written work should be a mirror-like reflection of the logic that is used for an author to effectively argue or present the main point of that work. Any imposition or interruption in the logical flow will be perceived by readers as evidence that the author's writing lacks the necessary focus. Authors are encouraged to abide by the following rules for developing and maintaining the necessary flow:

- **Construct Natural Progression:** All forms of scholarly writing report on something new. That new information, whether it is a case study, a research report, or a theoretical work, was generated as a result of a natural sequence of events and thought. Authors must follow that sequence as they relate their experience in writing.
- **Avoid Traps:** Do not allow the order of discovery to interrupt the logical flow of the argument or presentation; this is a common trap for authors who are reporting on the results of original research. Furthermore, do not allow quality of evidence, no matter how compelling it may be, to dictate the organization of the written work. Evidence is far more persuasive when it is given within the natural sequence of an author's argument or presentation.
- **Maintain Relevance:** Make certain that every part of the written work pertains directly to the main point; this is particularly important for scholarly papers. Every part of an author's work—the title, the sections, and every paragraph therein—should relate to the main point. No matter how eloquent they may seem, irrelevant passages will interrupt the flow, and they should be stricken.
- **Maintain Balance:** Make certain that sections of the written work are presented evenly. Be certain to address each individual point with equal vigor. Relevant examples and implications should be developed equally for each point.

Parallel Structure

Authors must develop a unifying organization to their work that readers will recognize from section to section and from start to finish. Commonly known as parallel structure, this element of academic writing relates to the continuity of presented ideas, and also to the consistent manner by which ideas are presented. As noted, the organization of an author's work must follow the logic of their argument or presentation. The principle of parallel structure holds that the same organization must be present from section to section of that work. Furthermore, parallel structure requires a consistent form of presentation, and a consistent deployment of writing mechanics.

Parallel Sections. Authors should present ideas in the same manner and order throughout the course of their work. As an example, authors of research papers should report their data based on the order dictated by their original hypotheses; in turn, this information should drive the order of presentation in the following discussion and conclusion sections. This builds continuity of text, it generates momentum for the author's argument or presentation, and it results in improved reader comprehension and satisfaction. Discontinuity of presented ideas is confusing and frustrating to readers, and it weakens the overall impact of an author's work.

Parallel Form. Headings, subheadings, figures, lists, or any other forms of presenting ideas must be consistent throughout the course of a written work in terms of design, placement, and purpose. As an example, a series of tables created to highlight research results should include the same design conventions, they should be similarly placed in proximity to related text, and they should be created for the purpose of illuminating significant aspects of a study. Inconsistent form creates imbalance, it compromises the effectiveness of an author's argument or presentation, and it is regarded by editors and reviewers as a matter of sloppiness. Authors must also take care to avoid instances of imposed or unnatural form, such as the use of unnecessary headings, subheadings, figures, or lists. Form should be dictated primarily by the function of the author's argument or presentation, and to a limited extent, by requirements from individual publishers or publications.

Parallel Mechanics. The use of narration, grammar, punctuation, and vocabulary must be consistent throughout the course of a written work. This rule of parallel structure relates closely to the fundamentals of writing, to which countless volumes of text are already devoted. However, it is important emphasize that inconsistencies in writing mechanics are among the most common mistakes found in LIS manuscripts. For example, authors may change their form of address in a written work, they may mismatch the tenses, they may alternate between the uses of different forms of punctuation to highlight ideas, or they may vacillate between older and more contemporary terminologies. Such examples of inconsistent mechanics are confusing to the reader, they compromise the effectiveness of an author's argument or presentation, and like inconsistent form, they are regarded by editors and reviewers as matters of sloppiness. Relative to this point, authors must also take care to avoid redundancy. This is particularly pertinent to the use of vocabulary. Overuse of words and phrases quickly becomes monotonous to the reader, and it suggests a lack of author sophistication.

Length and Breadth

The organization of one's work is also reflected in its length and breadth. Authors are encouraged to abide by a recurring principle in this text: form follows function. Here, this means that the length of one's manuscript should be dictated primarily by the nature of its subject matter. To a limited degree, the requirements of individual publishers and publications can also dictate length. As a general rule, however, authors should provide enough text to emphasize the main point of their work, and they should avoid any unnecessary, gratuitous, or repetitive language. Similarly, authors are discouraged from including any subject matter that is not pertinent to the main topic. As with insufficient or unnecessary coverage of the main topic, the inclusion of unrelated subject matter is a result of unfocused writing.

2.3 Style

Authors must write in a clear and precise style to effectively communicate their ideas. Hernon and Metoyer-Duran's (1993) seminal study in this area showed that clarity and precision are deemed by LIS scholars to be the most important attributes in academic writing. Authors must also establish continuity of ideas throughout the course of their work, they must maintain an even, economical, and uninterrupted flow, and they must use a professional tone. Finally, authors must present their ideas in a formal narrative style, and at the same time develop a personal style that effectively engages their readers and distinguishes their work in the field.

Clarity

Clarity is not easily defined in this context; it involves numerous essential elements of the academic writing process, all of which must be present and effectively applied. These elements can be distilled down and organized into the broad, descriptive categories below, all of which are discussed in detail in relevant sections of this text. Academic writing is clear when:

- It includes factual or speculative information that is relative to the main point of the author's work and nothing else;
- It is organized around the main point of the author's work and nothing else;
- It is presented in language that is easy for the intended audience to understand;
- It follows the standards of writing mechanics.

Authors are encouraged to use the following strategies for improving the overall clarity of their writing:

- **Read the work aloud** while revising and editing. This helps authors to identify flaws in their own work that might not be as apparent through silent editing.
- **Share the work with colleagues** who have published in the same field. Sharing with more than one colleague is highly recommended; their differing and overlapping feedback is essential for identifying the particular strengths and weaknesses in one's writing.
- **Allow the work to sit idle** for a day. A fresh or rested perspective is often necessary for improved writing, revising, and editing.

Precision

In this context, precision relates to the selection and use of vocabulary in one's writing. Authors must make certain that every word is selected and used to communicate ideas exactly as they intend. The following elements of precision are identified as particular areas of concern for LIS authors:

Word Selection. Use words that best communicate intended ideas. Authors commonly use words that fit loosely in the context of their work. It is vital to remember that every written word has both general and specific meanings, and sometimes even subtle insinuations. Poor word selection significantly weakens an author's argument or presentation. This is particularly true for verb choice, but it applies to all elements of the constructed sentence.

EXAMPLE: Word Selection

IMPRECISE: The purpose of this study is to **tell...**

PRECISE: The purpose of this study is to **demonstrate...**

IMPRECISE: The authors **executed** a thorough literature review...

PRECISE: The authors **conducted** a thorough literature review...

IMPRECISE: Information science is an interdisciplinary **area...**

PRECISE: Information science is an interdisciplinary **field...**

Word Economy. Use only the words that are necessary to communicate ideas. Eliminate any and all unnecessary language.

EXAMPLE: Word Economy

INCORRECT: **The reason why she scheduled library instruction** for her students **was to** show them the relevant engineering databases.

CORRECT: **She scheduled library instruction** for her students to show them the relevant engineering databases.

INCORRECT: **For the purpose of soliciting** survey respondents, the authors...

CORRECT: **To solicit** survey respondents, the authors...

Word Sophistication. Use appropriate vocabulary for an audience of professional peers. However, avoid the common trap of using pedantic or unnecessarily decorative vocabulary.

EXAMPLE: Word Sophistication

INCORRECT: College administrators perceive the role of library faculty as **being less important**...

CORRECT: College administrators perceive the role of library faculty as **ancillary**...

INCORRECT: There is **a scarce supply** of information on academic presses that **put out** new LIS books each year...

CORRECT: There is a **dearth** of information on academic presses that **publish** new LIS books each year...

INCORRECT: The authors **propose potential ameliorations**...

CORRECT: The authors **suggest ways to improve**...

Word Repetition: Avoid overuse of words and phrases. Be particularly cognizant of repetitive subject and character usage, and the overuse of articles (i.e., "a," "the") and prepositions (i.e., "at," "in," "on," "of," "from"). Problems of repetition are often resolved by sentence restructuring and the proper deployment of clearly defined pronouns or synonyms.

EXAMPLE: Word and Phrase Redundancy

INCORRECT: **The authors** implemented the new lending policy. **The authors** believed it would eliminate inefficiencies in the system.

CORRECT: The authors implemented the new lending policy; **they** believed it would eliminate inefficiencies in the system.

INCORRECT: As **the** study showed, **the** use of **the** think-pair-share technique improved **the** learning outcomes of **the** students.

CORRECT: As **the** study showed, using **the** think-pair-share technique improved student learning outcomes.

Colloquialisms: Avoid use of informal words, phrases, and aphorisms. These errors of precision weaken the impact of an author's argument or presentation.

EXAMPLE: Colloquialisms

INCORRECT: The director's grant proposal was **dead on arrival.**

INCORRECT: In library web design, **less is more.**

General Statements and Approximations. Avoid use of broad, unsubstantiated statements and approximations. Be specific and provide the necessary evidence to support statements.

EXAMPLE: General Statements and Approximations

INCORRECT: **Deans of library schools believe** their faculty should be required to publish...

CORRECT: Recent studies show that deans of library schools believe their faculty should be required to publish...(Booth, 2012; Williams, 2009)

INCORRECT: **Quite a number** of library educators are required to publish...

CORRECT: Taddeo's (2007) survey of library educators shows that 87% of those with faculty status are required to publish...

Jargon. It is common for LIS practitioners to use the term "library jargon" in the context of professional vernacular that is confusing to library users. Library users, for instance, may be unfamiliar with the terms federated search, periodical database, or metadata. However, those users are not the intended readers of professional LIS literature. The intended readers are peers in the profession who appreciate and understand professional vernacular. This differs from the term "jargon" as it is used in the present context. Here, jargon is the unnecessarily complex manner of expressing simpler words or phrases. Jargon is generally regarded as confusing, discordant gibberish to readers, and it should be scrupulously avoided.

> ### *EXAMPLE:* Jargon
>
> *INCORRECT:* Affective library user cognitive and somatic behavior...
>
> *CORRECT:* Library anxiety...

Continuity

Effective academic writing includes continuity of presentation. Each sentence should fit logically and linguistically between previous and following sentences. There should be a flow in which ideas and language fit together, and through which there is a momentum of presented ideas. Continuity is commonly achieved by way of transitional devices such as pronoun substitution (e.g., "they" for "the authors"), and transitional words or phrases (e.g., "as a result," "furthermore," "conversely"). Authors are strongly encouraged to read their work aloud while writing and editing. This is an effective way of identifying interruptions in overall continuity.

> ### *EXAMPLE:* Continuity
>
> *CORRECT:* **Galvin's (2013) study** specifically addressed user needs in the area of extension services; **the results of his work** disproved many commonly held assumptions. **For this reason**, administrators are encouraged...

Non Sequiturs. The non sequitur is a sentence or statement that has no apparent logical relevance to the previous sentence or statement. This error is usually corrected by using a transitional device, or by removing the irrelevant text.

EXAMPLE: Non Sequitur

INCORRECT: Download statistics demonstrate the need to improve the marketing strategy for e-books. The authors implemented a new policy.

CORRECT: Download statistics demonstrate the need to improve the marketing strategy for e-books. **As a result,** the authors implemented a new policy.

Tone

The nature and purpose of academic writing requires that authors establish a professional tone. Authors are expected to present their work in a civil, direct, honest, level, and measured fashion. This does not mean that academic writing should be tedious or uninteresting, nor does it mean that authors are precluded from developing a personal style. Instead, authors should equate the tone of their writing to a form of professional behavior, and they should present their work accordingly. The following elements of tone are identified as particular areas of concern for LIS authors:

Antagonism. Scholarly discourse brings together authors with differing, and sometimes opposing viewpoints. Although the discourse in LIS is comparatively benign, authors will sometimes disagree with or find shortcomings in one another's work. In such instances, it is vital to maintain an engaged, but professional tone.

EXAMPLE: Avoiding Antagonistic Tone

INCORRECT: Gramlich and Miller's (2011) study **completely ignores...**

> ### *EXAMPLE:* Avoiding Antagonistic Tone, cont.
>
> *CORRECT:* The authors believe that Gramlich and Miller's (2011) study **does not account for...**

Defensiveness. Sometimes authors lack confidence in their own work; this is particularly common for those who are inexperienced. These authors tend to compensate for their lack of confidence in two ways: They overemphasize the supporting evidence to the point of including unnecessary or irrelevant information, and they underemphasize the noteworthiness of their own work by way of indirect statements and tentative assertions. Writing confidently is critical to establishing a professional tone.

> ### *EXAMPLE:* Avoiding Defensive Tone
>
> *INCORRECT:* As shown in Figure 3, survey respondents—**including 42 undergraduate and 23 graduate students—overwhelmingly** regard the library...
>
> *CORRECT:* As shown in Figure 3, **94% of survey respondents** regard the library...
>
> *INCORRECT:* Results of the survey **seem to show...**
>
> *CORRECT:* Results of the survey **show...**

Dogmatism. As noted, scholarly discourse brings together authors with opposing viewpoints. Authors should acknowledge these differences in their own work. It is not necessary to devote substantial portions of one's work to opposing views, but it is important to include the thrust of them as leverage for an author's own argument or presentation.

EXAMPLE: Avoiding Dogmatic Tone

While Hood and Jankowski (2005) argue that it is unnecessary to maintain a regularly staffed reference desk in the campus library, the author of the present study demonstrates...

Narration

The standard form of address in academic writing is formal. Informality defeats the main purpose of academic writing, which is to communicate information in a clear, direct, and succinct way. To establish formality, authors must use third-person narration, which requires that they refer to themselves as "the author(s)" or by an equivalent term, and that they use relative pronouns (e.g., it, his, her, their, them, they). Although the commonly required style manuals for LIS professionals make some allowances for the use of nominative first-person narration (e.g., he, she, we), the general standard is third-person. This can be an awkward form of address, because if forces authors into unnatural modes of expression. To overcome this, authors must develop a personal style that abides by standards of formal writing, communicates necessary ideas, and effectively engages the reader. This requires practice.

EXAMPLES: Formal Narrative Style (Third-Person)

CORRECT: **The authors** attribute the success of this case study to...

CORRECT: The library environment in which **the researchers** conducted this study...

CORRECT: As a result of the **author's** proposed changes, **her** colleagues are...

Personal Style

There is more to effective academic writing than simply following the rules contained in this text or others. Authors should work to develop a personal style of academic writing that demonstrates a connection to the subject matter that is being argued or presented. Readers will find the resulting work to be more interesting, and even more compelling. The author of the present text recommends the following strategies for developing a personal style:

- Emulate the work of LIS authors who have an engaging writing style. Pay particular attention to the manner by which these authors establish clarity, precision, continuity, and tone.
- Compose as if writing for one specific reader instead of a broader audience of peers. It is easier to experiment with personal style when arguing or presenting the main subject matter with only one reader in mind.

2.4 **Mechanics**

Mechanics relate to the fundamental tools of written communication that authors must master in order to effectively communicate their ideas. This section of the text is devoted primarily to issues concerning grammar, but necessary attention is also given to punctuation, spelling, capitalization, and abbreviation. The reader is reminded that the purpose of this section is not to substitute for any of the existing authoritative and comprehensive writing manuals, but rather to address the elements of writing mechanics that are identified as particular areas of concern for LIS authors.

2.4.1 Grammar

Grammar is the set of rules that governs how words are put together for the purpose of constructing proper and meaningful sentences. Grammatical mistakes equate to poor writing, which is cited as one of the primary reasons for LIS manuscript rejections (Hernon, Smith, & Croxen, 1993). As noted above, a group of experts in the field was consulted for the purpose of identifying the necessary information to be included in this section of the text. The most commonly identified grammatical concerns with LIS manuscripts are organized into the following categories: verbs, adverbs, pronouns, adjectives, prepositions, and conjunctions. The concerning elements of each grammatical category are addressed below, including examples and recommended solutions.

Verbs

Verbs are the most important communicators in all forms of writing; they denote actions or existence, and as such, they give life to sentences. The selection of appropriate verbs to relate specific actions or existence is vital, as noted above, but the correct use of verbs to construct sentences is equally important. The following are identified as the most common concerns related to the use of verbs in LIS manuscripts:

Active vs. Passive Voice. Voice pertains to whether the subject of a sentence acts or is acted on; the former of these is active voice, and the latter is passive. Active voice is preferred in academic writing. Passive voice is permitted in some instances of expository writing when authors wish to emphasize the subject as a recipient of an action, or when they wish to accentuate a particular point of view. As a general rule, however, passive voice is discouraged.

EXAMPLE: Active vs. Passive Voice

PASSIVE: **The manuscript was rejected** by the editors...

ACTIVE: **The editors rejected** the manuscript...

PASSIVE: **The pre-1985 bound periodicals will be removed** from the stacks on the library's third floor by student assistants.

ACTIVE: **Students assistants will remove** the pre-1985 bound periodicals from the stacks on the library's third floor.

Tense. Tense pertains to the time of actions or conditions: past, present, or future. Past tense is identified as the most problematic for LIS authors. The key to selecting appropriate tense for past actions or conditions is whether or not the action or condition occurred or existed at a specific time. For specific times in the past, authors should use past tense. For unspecific times in the past, or for descriptions of continuing actions, authors should use present perfect tense.

EXAMPLE: Applying Tense to Past Actions or Conditions

INCORRECT: Research from Senglaup (2011) **proves**...

CORRECT: Research from Senglaup (2011) **proved**...

INCORRECT: Since then, information scientists **worked** to...

CORRECT: Since then, information scientists **have worked** to...

Tense Confusion. Tense confusion occurs when authors unwittingly or unnecessarily shift tenses in a sentence or passage, or from paragraph to paragraph. This commonly occurs in sentences that are unnecessarily long or complex, or when they are constructed in a passive voice. Authors are encouraged to simplify sentences, and to write in an active voice.

EXAMPLE: Tense Confusion

INCORRECT: The lesson plan **requires** that librarians **demonstrate** the database for students who **asked** questions during the workshop.

CORRECT (PASSIVE): The lesson plan **requires** that librarians **demonstrate** the database for students who **ask** questions during the workshop.

CORRECT (ACTIVE): The workshop lesson plan **requires** librarians to **demonstrate** the database for students who **ask** questions.

Dangling Modifiers (Infinitives, Participles, and Gerunds). Modifiers are the words and phrases that give description in sentences. Three types of modifiers are identified as problematic for LIS authors: infinitives, participles, and gerunds. Infinitives are verb forms that usually consist of the word *to*, followed by a verb. However, infinitives are not used as verbs; instead, they function as a nouns, adjectives, or adverbs (e.g., to drink). Participles are derived from verbs; they modify nouns, and they can function as adjectives. A present participle, which invariably ends in *-ing*, attributes action to the noun (e.g., **Looking** back, one can see …). A past participle, which usually ends in *-ed*, views the noun as having undergone the action expressed by the participle (e.g., The librarian is commonly **perceived** as …). Like present participles, gerunds are also derived from verbs, and they invariably end in *–ing*. However, gerunds function as nouns (e.g., Administrators do not appreciate my **teaching.**).

When any of the modifiers above lack the necessary syntactical connection to the nearest subject in a given sentence, they are danglers. A sentence with a dangling modifier is perceived as illogical, or even incoherent to readers. This type of writing error is often the result of using passive voice, and it is corrected by restructuring the sentence in order to make it active.

EXAMPLE: Dangling Modifiers

INCORRECT: To improve her teaching, a different lesson plan was used.

CORRECT: She improved her teaching by using a different lesson plan.

INCORRECT: After a semester of Spanish language instruction, he was able to understand Latino library patrons better.

EXAMPLE: Dangling Modifiers, cont.

CORRECT: He was able to understand Latino library patrons better after a semester of Spanish language instruction.

Subject and Verb Agreement. Subject and verb agreement relates to the use of singular or plural word forms. As a general rule, a singular subject requires a singular verb, and a plural subject requires a plural verb. Elements of this rule can be confusing to authors. For example, multiple subjects that are connected by the words *or* or *nor*, and collective subjects that convey unity require singular verbs (e.g., The **university is** closed for…). Conversely, collective subjects that convey plurality require plural verbs (e.g., **Library faculty are** accustomed to…). The key to proper usage is to identify whether the subject is singular or plural, regardless of any intervening language, and then to form the verb accordingly.

EXAMPLE: Subject and Verb Agreement

INCORRECT: **The decision** to use circulation statistics for changing hours of operation **require** close scrutiny.

CORRECT: **The decision** to use circulation statistics for changing hours of operation **requires** close scrutiny.

INCORRECT: The resulting **data shows** that…

CORRECT: The resulting **data show** that…

Verb Contractions. Verb contractions can make prose *sound* smooth and natural, and they can make reading more enjoyable. However, contractions represent an informal manner of address, and they are inappropriate for academic writing.

EXAMPLE: Verb Contractions

INCORRECT: Library school students **aren't** required to master a second language.

CORRECT: Library school students **are not** required to master a second language.

Adverbs

Adverbs are words used to describe, modify, or qualify verbs, adjectives, and in some instances, other adverbs; they most commonly occur as words ending in *-ly* (e.g., precisely, really, stubbornly). Adverbs can also be used as effective introductory or transitional devices (e.g., consequently, conversely, importantly, unfortunately). However, LIS authors are cautioned against unnecessary use of these words. Whereas the effective use of adverbs enhances continuity and flow, unnecessary use interrupts those vital elements of one's writing. Adverbs can often be removed without having an impact on the overall meaning, impact, or momentum of a given sentence.

EXAMPLE: Adverbs

INCORRECT: Although the study results showed improved student learning, the authors **actually** believe...

CORRECT: Although the study results showed improved student learning, the authors believe...

Pronouns

Pronouns are words used as substitutes for nouns, and in some instances, for other pronouns; they may be used as substitutes for expressed nouns or pronouns (e.g., **The library** is closed, but **it** will reopen soon.), and for unexpressed, but understood nouns (e.g., **It** is noisy in the computer classroom.). Proper usage requires authors to match pronouns with their antecedents in terms of case, gender, number and person. Effective usage is critical for avoiding repetitive language, particularly in academic writing. The following are identified as the most common concerns related to the use of pronouns in LIS manuscripts:

Personal Pronouns. Academic writing requires the use of third-person narration. In this context, personal pronouns indicate who or what is being referred to (e.g., **Their** research showed…). Authors have the following third-person narrative pronouns to operate with:

- *Nominative Singular:* he, she, it
- *Nominative Plural:* they
- *Objective Singular:* him, her, it
- *Objective Plural:* them
- *Genitive Singular:* his, her, hers, its
- *Genitive Plural:* their, theirs

Objective and genitive pronouns are preferred in academic writing; nominative pronouns are permissible, but discouraged. Use of the nominative plural *they* is discouraged because it avoids the directness and specificity that is required in academic writing, particularly with respect to known or unknown gender (see example below). Authors are also discouraged from using the third-person plural pronouns *they, them,* and *their* in reference to a singular antecedent; while this is generally accepted in forms of informal writing, it is considered grammatically incorrect and unacceptable for academic writing.

EXAMPLE: Third-Person Personal Pronouns

INCORRECT: I had access to the archival collection by virtue of **my** affiliation with the University.

CORRECT: **The author** had access to the archival collection by virtue of **her** affiliation with the University.

INCORRECT (KNOWN GENDER): **Study participant C** declined to sign the waiver because of **their**...

CORRECT (KNOWN GENDER): **Study participant C** declined to sign the waiver because of **his**...

INCORRECT (UNKNOWN GENDER): When **a potential survey responder** approached the circulation desk, **they** were greeted...

CORRECT (UNKNOWN GENDER): When **a potential survey responder** approached the circulation desk, **he or she** was greeted...

Editorial **We.** As noted, the commonly required style manuals for LIS professionals make allowances for the limited use of nominative first-person narration. The most commonly accepted first-person pronoun is the editorial *we,* which is used to refer to one's self and his or her co-author(s). The use of *we* is recommended for describing the necessary processes and procedures in one's work. Any use of *we* beyond that context is generally confusing to readers.

EXAMPLE: Editorial *We*

ACCEPTABLE: **The authors** explored three potential solutions...

ACCEPTABLE: **We** explored three potential solutions...

INCORRECT: **We** view the closing of undergraduate libraries as short-sighted...

CORRECT: **Directors from ARL institutions** view the closing of under-graduate libraries as shortsighted...

Unclear Antecedents. The unclear antecedent is an unknown subject to which a pronoun refers. This type of writing error is identified as a very common mistake in LIS manuscripts. It is confusing to the reader, and it interrupts the overall flow. The unclear antecedent is easily corrected by providing more specific information about the subject that is referred to.

EXAMPLE: Unclear Antecedent

INCORRECT: Students do not use the music library because **they** do not have enough computer workstations.

CORRECT: Students do not use the music library because **that facility** does not have enough computer workstations.

Relative Pronouns. A relative pronoun introduces a dependent clause and connects it to an independent clause in the same sentence. The most commonly used relative pronouns are *who, what, which,* and *that.* As an example, the sentence, "This is the book that Kate recommends," is comprised of the independent clause, "This is the book ...," and the dependent clause, "...that Kate recommends," and the two clauses are connected by the relative pronoun *that*.

The most commonly identified concern with relative pronouns is the confusion caused by mismatching their recommended uses. *Who* refers to a person; *which* usually refers to a thing; *what* typically refers to a nonliving thing; and *that* refers to a person or thing. The confusion over sentences with *that* and *which* clauses is a particular concern. There is a general rule to guide the use of these relative pronouns. *That* clauses are restrictive; they define the subject in a sentence (e.g., These are the results **that** show...). *Which* clauses are unrestrictive; they relate additional, incidental, or qualifying information about the subject in a sentence (e.g., These are the results, **which** show...). This general rule also holds that *which* clauses require the use of a preceding comma, and *that* clauses do not.

EXAMPLE: Relative Pronouns

INCORRECT: Those are the information scientists **that** proved...

CORRECT: Those are the information scientists **who** proved...

RESTRICTIVE: Soom (2008) presented evidence **that** negated...

NONRESTRICTIVE: Soom (2008) presented evidence, **which** negated...

Possessive Pronouns. A possessive pronoun is used as an adjective to qualify a noun in a sentence (e.g., **His** research on museum collections...). Standards of academic writing stipulate that authors should use only third-person possessive pronouns. This qualifies the use of *his, her, hers, its,* and *their,* and disqualifies the use of *my, mine, our, ours, your,* and *yours.* Although the use of possessive pronouns is acceptable in academic writing, authors are encouraged to avoid overuse. Incorrect use of *its* is identified as a common mistake in LIS manuscripts. This error occurs when authors confuse *its*, the possessive pronoun, with *it's*, the contraction of *it is*.

EXAMPLE: Possessive Pronouns

INCORRECT: Results of **our** work with homeless patrons may have implications for **your** library...

CORRECT: Results of **the authors'** work with homeless patrons may have implications for **other libraries**...

INCORRECT: Researchers should consider the comparatively high cost of this instrument, and also the implications of **it's** use...

CORRECT: Researchers should consider the comparatively high cost of this instrument, and also the implications of **its** use...

Misplaced Adjectives

Adjectives are words that qualify or describe nouns or noun phrases in a given sentence (e.g., **short** presentation; **powerful** documentary; **disturbing** behavior); they are used to describe number, possession, size, type, or any other qualifying information relative to its subject in a sentence. The most commonly identified concern regarding the use of adjectives in LIS manuscripts relates to their improper placement in sentences. The general rule for placement holds that an adjective usually precedes its qualifying object. However, there are notable exceptions. An adjective may follow the qualifying noun or noun phrase when particular emphasis is necessary (e.g., food **aplenty**), when standard usage requires it (e.g., Attorney **General**), or when it is a predicate that follows a linking verb (e.g., The library washrooms smell **bad**). An adjective is misplaced if it follows its qualifying object, but does not meet with any of these criteria.

EXAMPLE: Misplaced Adjectives

INCORRECT: O'Brien's (2011) work showed that ESL students who use library source materials **rarely** are more likely to struggle with...

CORRECT: O'Brien's (2011) work showed that ESL students who **rarely** use library source materials are more likely to struggle with...

Prepositions and Prepositional Phrases

A preposition is a word or phrase that connects an object to an antecedent and elucidates the relationship between them. Most often the object is a noun, and the relationship relates to direction, time, or location (e.g., I took a shuttle **to** the south campus; The student rummaged **through** her backpack; He daydreamt **during** the committee meeting). By extension, a prepositional phrase consists of a proposition, its relative object, and any relative object qualifiers (e.g., The alarm sounded **after the third period**; New book jackets are posted **on the green kiosk**). The following are identified as the most common concerns related to the use of prepositions and prepositional phrases in LIS manuscripts:

Ending with a Preposition. Although traditional rules of English language usage caution against ending sentences with prepositions, authors are permitted to do so. It is often necessary to end with a preposition to avoid an unnecessarily convoluted sentence. For example, the sentence, "These are the behaviors I warned you **about**," ends appropriately. Restructuring the sentence to avoid ending with a preposition is awkward: "These are the behaviors **about** which I warned you." However, authors are encouraged to avoid the common mistake of ending a sentence with an unnecessary preposition, as demonstrated below:

EXAMPLE: Ending with a Preposition

INCORRECT: The school year is over **with**.

CORRECT: The school year is over.

INCORRECT: Where is she walking **to**?

CORRECT: Where is she walking?

Preposition Overuse. Preposition overuse is another common error found in LIS manuscripts; this tends to occur in sentences that are too long or unnecessarily complex. The general rule for avoiding overuse is to maintain a separation of at least ten words between prepositions in the same sentence, particularly when the same word is used. The exception to this rule is a sentence that includes a series of items, each requiring use of the same preposition, or preferably, different ones (e.g., He searched **through** the stacks, **in** the book return bin, and **around** the re-shelving area). Preposition overuse can also be avoided by maintaining a clear and simple sentence structure and by writing in an active voice.

EXAMPLE: Ending with a Preposition

INCORRECT: The authors were **in** constant communication **with** the Human Subjects Department **in** an effort **to** avoid conflicts **of** interest **in** the study.

CORRECT: **To** avoid conflicts **of** interest **in** the study, the authors maintained constant communication **with** the Human Subjects Department.

Unnecessary Prepositions. The English language includes numerous nouns that are derived from verbs; they commonly end in *-ance, -ence, -ity, -ment, -sion,* and *-tion* (e.g., the noun **instruction** is derived from the verb **instruct**). Sentences with these nouns often require the use of prepositions (e.g., Online **instruction** is necessary **for** librarians **to** demonstrate...). In such instances, the preposition can often be eliminated and the sentence can be simplified by using the appropriate verb form (e.g., Librarians **instruct** online **to** demonstrate...).

Unnecessary Prepositional Phrases. In some sentences strong adverbs can substitute for weak or unnecessary prepositional phases. For example, the sentence "Our history librarian **searched with rigor**," is more effectively written, "Our history librarian searched **rigorously**." Appropriate genitives, particularly those that involve the preposition *of,* can also substitute for weak or unnecessary prepositional phrases. For example, the sentence, "The Circulation Manager was annoyed by the **attitude of the computer support** technician," is more effectively written, "The **computer support technician's attitude** annoyed the Circulation Manager."

Conjunctions

Conjunctions are words or phrases that connect clauses or words within a clause; the most common conjunctions are *and, but, if, or,* and *so*. Compound conjunctions are also single words, but they are formed by the combination of multiple words; the most common of these are *although, because,* and *unless*. Phrasal conjunctions, which are less commonly used, are made up of multiple words; examples include *as though, so that,* and *supposing that*. The following are identified as the most common concerns related to the use of conjunctions in LIS manuscripts:

Beginning Sentences with Conjunctions. Standard style manuals used by LIS professionals allow for authors to begin sentences with conjunctions, and therefore, to connect sentences with them. With few exceptions, however, that usage is considered informal in the context of academic writing, and it is discouraged. The most formal and commonly accepted sentence-beginning conjunctions in scholarly writing are *albeit* and *however*. Similar use of *although, since,* and *while* is generally permitted, but that is subject to editorial preferences. As a general rule, authors who are inclined to begin sentences with informal conjunctions are encouraged to make use of the following substitutions:

- For *and,* use *also* or *in addition*
- For *because,* use *as a result* or *consequently*
- For *but,* use *however*
- For *or,* use *otherwise*
- For *so,* use *as a result* or *consequently*

Conjunction Overuse. Like preposition overuse, conjunction overuse is a common error tending to occur in sentences that are too long or unnecessarily complex. Unlike preposition overuse, there is no general rule for avoiding overuse in terms of a suggested number of words to separate them by in the same sentence. It is recommended, however, that authors avoid repetitive use of the same conjunction in the same sentence. This can be avoided by reading one's work aloud to detect repetitive flaws, and by maintaining a clear and simple sentence structure.

EXAMPLE: Conjunction Overuse

INCORRECT: The author **and** editor commenced with their collaboration, **and** they frequently corresponded **and** conferred on the project **and** its implications.

CORRECT: The author **and** editor commenced with their collaboration; they frequently corresponded **and** conferred on the project **and** its implications.

CORRECT: The author **and** editor commenced with their collaboration. They frequently corresponded **and** conferred on the project **and** its implications.

Subordinate Conjunctions. Subordinate conjunctions connect clauses of differing importance in a sentence. For this type of sentence there is an independent clause that can stand alone as its own sentence, and a subordinate clause that cannot stand alone. As an example, the sentence, "Search the database until you find it," is comprised of the independent clause, "Search the database...," and the subordinate clause "...until you find it," and the two clauses are connected by the subordinate conjunction *until*. The most commonly identified concern with subordinate conjunctions in LIS manuscripts is the confusion over appropriate uses of *since* and *while*, and their substitutes, *although, and, because,* and *but*.

***Use of* Since *and* While.** Authors are strongly encouraged to limit their use of *since* and *while* to references of time (e.g., Cindy has not taught **since**...; Testing was administered **while** the authors...). Although the standard style manuals used by LIS professionals allow for uses of *since* and *while* in a manner that does not refer to time, it is inaccurate to do so, it is confusing to the reader, and it is generally discouraged. When the word *since* is used in reference to something other than time, *because* should be substituted. Similarly, when the word *while* is used in reference to something other than time, *although, and,* and *but* should be substituted.

EXAMPLE: Use of *Since* and *While*

INCORRECT: No actions were taken **since** the public library's Board of Trustees was politically appointed.

CORRECT: No actions were taken **because** the public library's Board of Trustees was politically appointed.

INCORRECT: **While** library administrators disagree with campus police policies, they abide by them.

CORRECT: **Although** library administrators disagree with campus police policies, they abide by them.

2.4.2 *Punctuation*

Punctuation is the standardized system of symbols used by writers to clarify their work in terms of emphases, intonations, pauses, and stops. The recurring theme of this text—form follows function—applies to the use of punctuation, too. That is, punctuation use should be guided by its ultimate function, which is to facilitate the ease of reading. As with all elements of writing, punctuation involves a measure of subjectivity on behalf of the author and the reader. Since the purpose of academic writing is to communicate scholarly ideas clearly and precisely, it is the author's responsibility to limit subjectivity by using punctuation in a consistent, logical, and simple manner. The following are identified as the most common concerns related to the use of punctuation in LIS manuscripts:

Commas

The comma indicates a small break in a sentence; it is used mainly to distinguish between independent and subordinate clauses, to separate independent clauses connected by a conjunction, to separate items in a list or series, and to add stylistic pauses. The comma is identified as the most commonly concerning punctuation mark in LIS manuscripts. Authors are encouraged to review and abide by the following rules:

Run-on Sentences. Readers of this text are reminded that clarity and precision are essential for effective academic writing. The sophisticated nature of ideas in scholarly writing often requires a complex manner of presentation, and as a result, authors will sometimes attempt to fit too much information into a single sentence. This is the run-on sentence; it occurs when the author unnecessarily prolongs the sentence with added commas. The run-on sentence is confusing to the reader, and it must be scrupulously avoided.

EXAMPLE: Run-on Sentence

INCORRECT: Sixty-eight percent of the students submitted their midterm examination answers electronically, however the author continued to use the university's unwieldy courseware platform because anecdotal evidence suggested that students preferred this manner of participation, and also because the practical nature of moving to a print-based method of assessing student progress would have been too labor-intensive, particularly at mid-semester.

CORRECT: Sixty-eight percent of the students submitted their midterm examination answers electronically. However, the author continued to use the university's unwieldy courseware platform because anecdotal evidence suggested that students preferred this manner of participation, and also because the practical nature of moving to a print-based method of assessing student progress would have been too labor-intensive, particularly at mid-semester.

Comma Overuse. Authors must take care to avoid the very familiar error of overusing commas. This typically occurs in poorly constructed sentences that begin with adverbial clauses, participle phrases, infinitives, infinitive phrases, or prepositional phrases. To avoid this, authors should remake their sentences into clearer and simpler ones, and they should remember to present their ideas in an active voice. Overuse is also common in sentences where authors unnecessarily insert commas to set off restrictive words, phrases, or clauses. With this type of error, commas marginalize the antecedents of those words, phrases, or clauses.

> ### *EXAMPLE:* Comma Overuse
>
> *INCORRECT:* Until the authors received the results, they could not proceed.
>
> *CORRECT:* The authors could not proceed until they received the results.
>
> *INCORRECT:* To proceed, the authors needed the results.
>
> *CORRECT:* The authors needed the results to proceed.
>
> *INCORRECT:* Examples, like this, demonstrate the importance...
>
> *CORRECT:* Examples like this demonstrate the importance...
>
> *INCORRECT:* The researcher, who debunked that theory, continues to work...
>
> *CORRECT:* The researcher who debunked that theory continues to work...

Comma Splices. The comma splice occurs when an author separates independent clauses in a sentence with a comma, but neglects to include the appropriate connecting conjunction. Inserting the conjunction will correct the error, but a period or a semicolon can work with equal effectiveness.

> ### *EXAMPLE:* Comma Splice
>
> *INCORRECT:* Study participants received extra course credit, **they** were also given gift cards for their time.

CORRECT: Study participants received extra course credit, **and they** were also given gift cards for their time.

CORRECT: Study participants received extra course credit. **They** were also given gift cards for their time.

CORRECT: Study participants received extra course credit; **they** were also given gift cards for their time.

Commas to Separate Three or More Items. As a rule, commas should be used to separate all three or more items included in a sentence list or series. Importantly, this rule applies to the last item in the list or series, which typically follows a conjunction (i.e., *and, or*).

EXAMPLE: Commas to Separate Three or More Items

INCORRECT: Brower (2012) showed the scholarly, **economic and** philosophical benefits of open access...

CORRECT: Brower (2012) showed the scholarly, **economic, and** philosophical benefits of open access...

Semicolons

As a rule, the semicolon is used to separate two independent clauses that are not already connected by a conjunction; it can also be used to separate items in a list or series if those items also include internal punctuation. When used to separate independent clauses, the second clause typically includes the use of a pronoun with a clearly identified antecedent. This helps to maintain the intended momentum of constructing a compound sentence. The semicolon represents a stronger pause that a comma, but a weaker pause than a period. It also represents continuity from one clause to another, and from one series item to another. Misuse of the semicolon results in unnecessarily convoluted sentences, and it confuses readers.

EXAMPLE: Semicolons

CORRECT: The authors discontinued the focus group interviews; nevertheless, they were able to complete the study.

CORRECT: Hollander (2011) touted the vital nature of simple library web design; his work showed a strong correlation between design simplicity and library user satisfaction.

CORRECT: In the first study group, participants included Patron A, an undergraduate level psychology major; Patron B, a graduate level linguistics student; and Patron C, a graduate level archaeology student.

Colons

The colon indicates a strong break in a sentence. As a general rule, the colon introduces elements that amplify, exemplify, explain, illustrate, list, or prove that which precedes it. Importantly, the part of the sentence preceding the colon must be an independent clause. That is, it must be able to stand alone as a sentence. Clauses that follow the colon can be either complete or incomplete; when they are complete, the first word must begin with a capital letter.

EXAMPLE: Colons

INCORRECT: **Limitations of the study included:** a comparatively small research sample, recalcitrant faculty, and limited access to assessment data.

CORRECT: **Limitations of the study were as follows:** a comparatively small research sample, recalcitrant faculty, and limited access to assessment data.

INCORRECT: The voters overwhelmingly agreed: **the County Executive** failed the public library system.

CORRECT: The voters overwhelmingly agreed: **The County Executive** failed the public library system.

Dashes

The dash, also known as the em dash or extended hyphen, can be used to effectively represent an abrupt, qualifying interruption in the overall continuity of a sentence. Authors may use a pair of dashes to insert a necessary interruption in the body of a sentence, or they may use a single dash at the end of a sentence to clarify or qualify the preceding text. It is common in both instances for authors to follow the single or opening dash with transitional expressions like *for example, namely, to wit,* or *that is.* To maximize their impact, and to minimize any disruptions in the overall flow of one's work, authors should use dashes sparingly and judiciously.

EXAMPLE: Dashes

CORRECT: Two other titles from the previous study—*Australian Academic and Research Libraries and Herald of Library Science*—were removed because they are published outside of the United States.

CORRECT: The Head of Public Services has little tolerance for common instances of unprofessional behavior—for example, chronic tardiness and talking out of turn during unit meetings.

Quotation Marks

In academic writing, quotation marks are used to set off directly quoted materials, whether they are spoken or written; they can also be used to indicate the titles of other short works. The most commonly identified concerns for using quotes include the placement of relative punctuation, capitalization of relative text, indication of titles, indication of special terminology, and confusion over the use of single versus double quotation marks. Authors are encouraged to review and abide by the following rules and examples.

Direct Quotations. Directly quoted materials require the use of double quotation marks. The use of block quotations is an exception to this rule; the standard manuals of style used by LIS professionals each define block quotes differently, but they do not require the use of quotation marks for blocks of quoted text. Directly quoted materials require that ending punctuation is placed inside the concluding quotation mark; there are no exceptions. Most of the confusion over this rule arises when direct quotations ask a question, or when external punctuation is used for the purpose of constructing compound sentences. See the examples below for clarification.

Direct quotations are preceded by transitional punctuation—most commonly, a comma—when included in the body of a larger sentence, and they begin with a capital letter. When it is necessary to include multiple uses of the same direct quotation in the same sentence, the first quotation begins with a capital letter, and subsequent uses begin in lower case (with the exception of proper names).

EXAMPLE: Direct Quotations

CORRECT: As Schiller (2007) concluded, "More empirical evidence is needed to demonstrate the effectiveness of case study teaching."

CORRECT: Unexpectedly, "When will this test begin?" was the respondent's first question.

CORRECT: According the bylaws, "Librarians have the same professional responsibilities as teaching faculty."; therefore, librarians are
required to publish in refereed journals.

CORRECT: Study participant B responded, "The library interface looks
simple," and then shifted her tone to inquire, "but who is responsible
for the confusing language?"

Title Quotations. The titles of shorter scholarly works, such as book chapters and journal articles, should be presented in double quotation marks.
The titles of more significant works, such as books and journals, should be
presented in italics. Ending punctuation is placed inside the concluding
quotation mark, but with one exception: question marks are placed after
the concluding quotation mark in sentences that ask a question, but end
with quotes around a title.

EXAMPLE: Title Quotations

CORRECT: Wilder's (2005) article, "Information Literacy Makes All
the Wrong Assumptions," drew criticism and ire of the information
literacy community.

CORRECT: Wilder's (2005) article, "Information Literacy Makes All the
Wrong Assumptions," was published in the *Chronicle of Higher Education.*

CORRECT: Why was the information literacy community threatened
by Wilder's (2005) article, "Information Literacy Makes All the Wrong
Assumptions"?

Special Terminology Quotations. Authors may place double quotation marks around words or phrases alerting readers to coined, conceived, ironic, or other nonstandard use of those terms. Importantly, quotation marks may be used for the first appearance of special terminology only; subsequent appearances should appear without quotes.

EXAMPLE: Special Terminology Quotations

CORRECT: Numerous "problem patron" policies have been implemented.

INCORRECT: Numerous 'problem patron' policies have been implemented.

INCORRECT: Numerous *problem patron* policies have been implemented.

Single vs. Double Quotations. The only acceptable use of single quotation remarks in academic writing is to set off specified text inside a larger body of text that is already enclosed by double quotation marks.

EXAMPLE: Single vs. Double Quotations

CORRECT: Based on his 2010 study, Hartman asserted, "Reference librarians are more wary of 'the stapler question' than with needing to learn new computer applications."

2.4.3 Spelling

Conformity and correctness are identified as the most common concerns related to spelling in LIS manuscripts. In terms of conformity, the most commonly required manuals of style for LIS professionals recommend that authors abide by spelling standards set forth in the most current edition of *Merriam-Webster's Collegiate Dictionary* (University of Chicago, 2010; American Psychological Association, 2010). When the dictionary provides more than one spelling for a word, authors should use the first one listed (e.g., select *judgment* instead of *judgement*). When words do not appear in the dictionary, authors should consult publisher or publication requirements, and as a last resort, they should defer to sound professional judgment.

Although the ubiquitous use of word processing applications and spell-check features minimize instances of misspelling and misuse, those errors do occur, and they reflect badly on an author's work. Spell-check programs do not account for homonyms (e.g., *bough* vs. *bow*) or for commonly confused words (e.g., *its* vs. *it's*; *than* vs. *then*). Furthermore, these programs do not account for the correct spellings of proper names. This is a particular concern for academic writers who are required to cite the works of other scholars in support of their arguments or presentations. One of the most common spelling errors occurs when an author cites the work of another scholar in-text, and then spells that scholar's name differently in the bibliography. To mitigate this, authors can use automated bibliographic managers like *EndNote, RefWorks,* or *Zotero* (see the Organizing the Literature Review section) to export citations directly from bibliographic databases and to import them into their word processing documents. Another solution is to create a custom dictionary in one's word processing application and to enter in the proper names of cited authors. This will equip the spell-check feature to find instances of inconsistent spellings.

2.4.4 Capitalization

Inconsistency is identified as the most common concern related to capitalization in LIS manuscripts. The specific concern is inconsistent use of capitalization with respect to proper versus general nouns, and formal versus informal titles.

Proper vs. General Nouns. As a rule, the major words of specifically identified proper nouns require capitalization, and the accompanying articles, conjunctives, and prepositions should begin with lower case letters. Importantly, this rule also holds that general nouns should begin with lower case letters.

EXAMPLE: Capitalization of Proper vs. General Nouns

PROPER: The **American Library Association's Committee on Accreditation** granted a conditional accreditation to the **Department of Library and Information Studies' Master of Library Science Program**.

GENERAL: The **accrediting body** granted conditional accreditation to the **library school's graduate level program**.

PROPER: The plagiarism tutorial is available on the **World Wide Web**.

GENERAL: The plagiarism tutorial is **web-based**.

PROPER: The author's collaborator teaches the linguistics course, **LIN 414: History of the English Language**.

GENERAL: The author's collaborator teaches a linguistics course on the **history of the English language**.

PROPER: Branches of the **Buffalo and Erie County Public Library** experience higher rates of patronage during economic downturns.

GENERAL: Branches of the **local public library** experience higher rates of patronage during economic downturns.

Formal vs. Informal Titles. As a general rule, formal titles that are placed immediately before a person's name are capitalized. Formal titles of relatively high professional importance, but without a person's name, are also capitalized. Informal titles that are attributed to a person, or formal titles of lesser professional importance, begin with lower case letters.

EXAMPLE: Capitalization of Formal vs. Informal Titles

FORMAL: Those messages were forwarded to **the Library Web Site Manager, Scott Hollander**.

INFORMAL: Those messages were forwarded to **Scott Hollander, the manager of the library web site**.

CORRECT: **The Library Director** assigned those responsibilities to **the reference librarian** who was on duty.

2.4.5 *Abbreviation*

The nature of academic writing often requires the use of abbreviations; this is particularly true for LIS literature. In the context of academic writing, abbreviations are commonly used to substitute for names of groups (e.g., COA for Committee on Accreditation), institutions (e.g., LSU for Louisiana State University), organizations (e.g., PLA for Public Library Association), professional programs (e.g., SAILS for Standardized Assessment of Information Literacy Skills), professional vernacular (e.g., MeSH for medical subject headings), and research terminology (SR for stimulus response). When used properly and reasonably, abbreviations help to facilitate the readability of one's work. Conversely, improperly and unreasonably used abbreviations clutter one's work and confuse the reader. The following are identified as the most common concerns related to the use of abbreviations in LIS manuscripts:

Abbreviation Placement. Abbreviations should be introduced parenthetically after the first appearance of the text that they will replace thereafter. The exceptions to this rule apply to book titles, book chapter titles, journal article titles, and journal article abstracts; parenthetical abbreviations are too disrupting in these parts of written works. Furthermore, no sentence should begin with an abbreviation. When it is necessary to beginning a sentence with previously abbreviated text, it should be spelled out in full.

EXAMPLE: Abbreviation Placement

CORRECT: The **Association of College and Research Libraries (ACRL)** is the premier professional organization through which to advocate for necessary change. For this reason, the author joined **ACRL** and began...

INCORRECT: **IL** is defined as a skill set that allows...

CORRECT: **Information literacy (IL)** is defined as a skill set that allows...

Abbreviation Underuse and Overuse. Abbreviations must be justified by an appropriate number of relevant uses in the author's work. There is, for example, no justification for adding a parenthetical abbreviation if no further uses are required, or if only one use is required in a different section of the text. The general rule for the minimum number of uses is three for shorter works, such as book chapters and journal articles. There is no rule for larger works; authors must rely on reason and sound professional judgment.

Authors must also take care to avoid overuse of abbreviations. Repetitive use of the same abbreviation is perceived by readers as an indication of unfocused and unsophisticated writing. Overuse of different abbreviations is confusing and frustrating to readers. In both instances, the abbreviations are distracting, and they interrupt the flow and overall impact of the author's work. Authors can avoid these errors by effectively using synonyms and clearly identified pronouns, and by restructuring their sentences.

EXAMPLE: Abbreviation Overuse

NOT PREFERRED: Students in **CG-3** were required to participate in two **BIs**, which were designed around **ACRL's IL standards 1-2**. A post-test was administered to assess students' **IL** skills by way of using the **OPAC**.

PREFERRED: Students in **Control Group 3** were required to participate in two **library instruction sessions**, which were designed around **ACRL's Information Literacy (IL) Standards One and Two**. A post-test was administered to assess students' **IL** skills by way of using the **online catalog**.

3

Elements of the Scholarly Paper

Definition

The scholarly paper is a concise written work that is based on an author's original experimentation, research, or theory; it is written by an expert in a given field of practice or study, and it is intended for an audience of peers in that field. The scholarly paper is written and presented in a manner that follows scholarly tradition, which involves standard components and a prescribed order. These standard components are more than simple, academic conventions; they are used to ensure that the scholarly paper achieves its purpose of contributing new knowledge, and also to guide readers in their understanding and assessment what the author is arguing or presenting.

When published, the scholarly paper is commonly referred to as a peer-reviewed, refereed, or juried journal article. As these terms imply, the scholarly paper is ordinarily subjected to professional evaluation by peers who are experts in the particular field of practice or study that is discussed or presented in the work. The purpose of employing these experts is to judge whether or not the paper constitutes a unique, useful, and worthy contribution to the field's body of knowledge. If the paper is deemed to meet these criteria, then it is disseminated to the greater community of scholars in that field by way of publication in a scholarly journal.

Significance

Notwithstanding the distinction of the scholarly book, as a general rule, the publication of a paper in a prestigious journal is regarded as having more significance than most other forms of scholarship. This rule may vary, given the context of different disciplines, institutions, and relative measures of prestige, but it holds as a general statement among most scholars. This is particularly true for scholars in the social sciences, which includes the practice and discipline of library and information science (LIS).

The variables in place that give scholarly papers their prominence begin with the aforementioned practice of peer review. By virtue of the practice involving experts in a particular field, it provides a measure of authority, prestige, and trustworthiness to a given work that is more significant than with other forms of scholarship (see Peer Review section). Published articles also have the advantage of fast and efficient dissemination mechanisms, including individual and institutional journal subscriptions, disciplinary indexes and databases, and even the free web. Although the free web has changed the research and publication landscape significantly, authors will continue to publish their works in scholarly journals for the foreseeable future. This is because most academic authors operate within a system of appointment, promotion, and tenure that encourages or requires publication in scholarly journals, and also because journal publishers are advantageously situated to benefit from continuing to grow this lucrative enterprise (see Journal Publishers section).

Even with the review process, it generally takes less time to write, publish, and disseminate scholarly papers than it does to do the same for book-length works. As a result, published journal articles are considered to be the most current contributions to a discipline or field of study. Published journal articles also have more incorporated dimensions of correction than scholarly books. In manuscript form, the scholarly paper must pass through the processes of peer review, editing, and copyediting. Even then, errors of commission or omission do slip through, and they are sometimes discovered after publication. The publishers of scholarly journals recognize this reality and allow for necessary corrections by way of acknowledging mistakes in subsequent issues, or by publishing other authors' critiques of erroneous works.

Brief History

The roots of the scholarly paper, as we know it today, can be traced back to Europe during the mid-to-late seventeenth century. Until that time, communication between scholars depended primarily on personal correspondence and attendance at meetings of learned societies, and before that on personal contact through travel between universities (Manten, 1980). As European governments of the time began to recognize the link between economic prosperity and scientific and technological achievement, the memberships of learned societies increased, and the demand grew for a more advanced system of disseminating new ideas. As a result, the first scholarly journals were published in 1665; they were the French *Le Journal des Sçavans* and the English *Philosophical Transactions of the Royal Society of London* (Brown, 1972).

The subject matter presented in the first scholarly journals was of a general scientific nature; these publications were typically comprised of papers from the proceedings of learned societies. It was several decades before more specialized journals began to appear, most of which were devoted to medicine. By the end of the eighteenth century, however, journals were more specialized; numerous disciplines and areas of study were represented. Also by this time, it was a standard practice for scholarly papers to include illustrations, methodologies, and references, and for those works to undergo the formal peer review process (Belcher, 2009).

There was exponential growth in the number of scholarly journals during the nineteenth century. Valauskas (1997) explains that this was due to a combination of the increased specialization and diversification of scholarship and the advent of cheap wood pulp-based paper for inexpensive mass publication. As Bowman (1985) shows, the first English language scholarly journal that could be associated with libraries appeared during this era: *American Antiquarian Society Proceedings*. The journal began publication in 1849, and it included scholarly papers from art historians, rare book librarians, and antiquarian booksellers. The first English language journal devoted entirely to library scholarship was *The Library: The Transactions of the Bibliographical Society*; it began publication in 1889, two years following Melvil Dewey's establishment of the first library school at Columbia University (Miksa, 1988).

It is important for authors to know and understand the history of the scholarly paper and the evolution of how it is communicated, particularly in their own disciplines. This helps authors to recognize their place in the field, and appreciate the significance of contributing their own works. As Belcher (2009) emphasizes:

> The origin of journals in letter writing still shapes the form: academic journals are records of scholarly conversations and current concerns. It is wise to remember this origin when writing. To submit an article to an academic journal is to begin a correspondence. (p. 104)

3.1 *Standard Components of the Scholarly Paper*

As noted, the scholarly paper involves standard components in a prescribed order. These are forms of structure and organization that follow a scholarly tradition, and they are in place to ensure that the paper achieves its purpose and guides the reader. The standard formula for presenting one's work generally includes title, abstract, introduction, literature review, method, results, discussion, conclusion, references, and appendices. However, this formula should be regarded as less of a technical procedure and more of a general framework. That is to say, there are numerous variables that can have an impact on the necessary components and organization of any given manuscript.

The traditions of one's discipline or field of study may require the use a particular writing style, and that will be reflected in the relative professional literature. Whereas an electrical engineer may be required to format his or her manuscript according to guidelines from the Council of Science Editors (CSE) in *Scientific Style and Format: The CSE Manual for Authors, Editors, and Publishers,* a social researcher may need to format his or her work according to rules of the American Sociological Association (ASA) in the *ASA Style Guide.* Chicago Style, as set forth in the *Chicago Manual of Style,* is most commonly used in LIS literature. However, American Psychological Association (APA) Style, as set forth in the *Publication Manual of the American Psychological Association,* is increasingly used in the discipline.

The type of scholarly paper will commonly dictate its necessary components and its order; this is a classic application of form following function. A theoretical paper, for instance, is unlikely to require the same components as a research paper; the former will ordinarily have no need for a method or results section. Individual journals or their publishers may have additional stipulations in terms of the preparation and presentation of one's manuscript. They may, for instance, have recommended parameters for titles and abstracts; they may encourage or discourage the ordering or the subdividing of manuscript components; they may have their own in-house style for referencing sources; or they may have limits or rules for appendices. All this information is generally provided on a publication's web site or in the front or back matter of its print edition.

3.1.1 The Title

Authors must never forget that the title is the reader's first impression of a given work. The title should be a simple and concise summary of the main idea argued or presented in one's paper. It should be a succinct, almost terse, statement of the main topic and the variables or issues involved, but it should also be fully explanatory and understandable to the reader.

EXAMPLES: Title

Assessing the Effectiveness of Providing Virtual Reference Services at a Rural Community College

A Case Study on the Use of Classroom Clickers to Improve Student Learning Outcomes in Undergraduate Library Instruction

Since the scholarly paper is intended for an audience of peers in the field, modest use of disciplinary vernacular in the title is appropriate, expected, and even useful. However, gratuitously academic or pedantic language is a barrier to prospective readers. Authors are also discouraged from overuse of what they deem to be catchy colloquialisms or clever puns in the construction of compound titles, in which separate parts are separated by a colon. Although, this is a common practice for article titles in the social sciences, and with LIS literature in particular, it can come across as amateurish and unprofessional. That said, each journal has its own unique style, which is reflected in the titles of their published articles. Some journals actually have specific rules for the construction of manuscript titles. For example, it is stipulated that "A title of not more than 16 words should be provided," for the journal, *Library Hi Tech* (Emerald, 2012). In an effort to assess editorial preferences, authors are encouraged to review multiple issues of any journals they are considering.

3.1.2 *The Abstract*

An abstract is a concise, but thorough summary of the information presented in a scholarly paper. In essence, it is a hyper-condensed version of a paper's overall content. A well-crafted abstract serves numerous essential purposes in terms of writing, publishing, and researching. To begin, it provides potential readers with a quick overview, allowing them to decide whether or not they wish to read the entire work; this is a vital efficiency that is built into the research process. Better written and more compelling abstracts attract more readers, which leads to greater exposure, higher citation rates, and increased impact.

A well-crafted abstract is also a highly useful instrument for connecting with journal editors. When included in a query, the abstract quickly provides the necessary information for editors to determine whether or not the work is appropriate for a journal, and it can be the key component to generating their interest. A good abstract also helps authors to remain focused on the trajectory their own work, particularly during the writing and revising processes. Although many authors regard the abstract as an afterthought, they are strongly encouraged to regard their abstract as the proverbial seed from which their manuscript will grow and blossom.

The ingredients of a good abstract are the same as those of a good manuscript, except that they are distilled down to the bare, essential elements. For most LIS manuscripts, these are generally captured in one concisely written paragraph. The necessary ingredients are:

- *Topic:* What is the article about?
- *Purpose:* Why is the article necessary?
- *Method:* How was the project or study was conducted? How was the data collected?
- *Results:* What were the results?
- *Conclusions:* What conclusions can be drawn, and what are the implications?

The ingredients of a bad abstract are of equal importance. Authors should take care to avoid the common mistake of including unnecessary information, or that which fundamentally does not belong in an abstract. For example, authors should avoid introducing the topic of the manuscript; that is for the introduction section. Authors should state what they did, but not what they hope to accomplish. Very often authors include statements that begin with language similar to, "This paper intends to...," or "The authors wish to show..." Such language or statements must be scrupulously avoided. Authors are also discouraged from adding citations or footnotes, quotations, abbreviations and acronyms, or from including too much data. To reiterate, the abstract is the hyper-condensed version of a paper, but it is also the selling point. As asserted by the American Psychological Association (2010), "A well-prepared abstract can be the most important single paragraph in an article" (p. 26).

EXAMPLE: Abstract for Research Paper

This study analyzed 2005–2006 Web of Science bibliometric data from institutions belonging to the Association of Research Libraries (ARL) and corresponding ARL statistics to find any associations between indicators from the two data sets. Principal components analysis on 36 variables from 103 universities revealed obvious associations between size-dependent variables, such as institution size, gross totals of library measures, and gross totals of articles and citations. However, size-independent library measures did not associate positively or negatively with any bibliometric indicator. More quantitative research must be done to authentically assess academic libraries' influence on research outcomes. (Hendrix, 2010, p. 32)

EXAMPLE: Abstract for Case Study Paper

Like other college and university departments, academic libraries are increasingly expected to assess their services and facilities. This article describes an initial step in the development of a comprehensive assessment program for library instruction in the Brooklyn College Library. A pre- and post-quiz were developed based on the curriculum for a required library session in an introductory English composition course. The quizzes were designed to establish a baseline for student knowledge of information literacy as well as measure the effect of library instruction on student learning. We also sought to evaluate the suitability of the Blackboard learning management system for assessment of library instruction. Our discussion of the benefits and limitations of this pilot project will be useful to instruction librarians considering using Blackboard to implement multiple choice quizzes as a means of assessing information literacy and library instruction. (Smale & Regaldo, 2009, p. 142)

Many journals have specific rules for the construction, content, and presentation of abstracts. For example, the following language is included in the author instructions for the journal, *portal: Libraries and the Academy*: "Include an abstract of no more than 100 words highlighting the scope, methodology, and conclusions of the paper. These are vital because they provide the keywords for searching the full text of the articles" (Johns Hopkins, 2012). Furthermore, some LIS journals require that authors develop a structured abstract, which includes distinct, labeled sections for concise descriptions of different parts of the paper. As an example, the author instructions for the *Journal of the Medical Library Association* (Medical Library Association, 2013) stipulate that contributing authors must submit a structured abstract, including separate categories for objective, methods, results, conclusions, and implication. To be certain, most journals also have their own unique style; this will be reflected in the abstracts of their published articles. Authors are encouraged to review multiple issues of the journals they are considering to assess editorial preferences.

3.1.3 *The Introduction*

Since the purpose of a scholarly paper is to contribute new knowledge, it requires an introduction in which the author presents a topic and describes an approach to addressing it. Most typically, the author presents a problem, and then describes a strategy for studying or solving it. This is true for most types of papers published in LIS journals: bibliographies, case studies, perspectives pieces, research articles, response articles, review articles, and theoretical articles. An effective introduction will successfully address the following in one-to-two pages of text:

- *Importance:* Why is the main topic or problem important to the discipline and to the reader?
- *Relativity:* Have other works been devoted to the same problem?
- *Noteworthiness:* How does the paper differ from other works?
- *Objective:* What does the author want to accomplish?
- *Method:* How does the author attempt to accomplish the objective?
- *Hypothesis:* How are the objective and method relative to one another?
- *Implications:* What does the main topic or problem mean for the discipline and for the reader?

EXAMPLE: Introduction

E-books have become more prevalent in academic library collections, yet the current literature suggests that academic users have not wholeheartedly embraced this format. Differences in the extent of e-book use are influenced by differences in academic disciplines. Much of the literature suggests that business researchers, a population composed of business students and faculty, were early and rapid adopters and continue to be heavy users of e-books. At the same time, other social sciences and humanities disciplines lag behind in their usage of e-books.

This article will explore the reasons why the usage rate of e-books is so consistently high for business researchers. The premise of this article is that the information-seeking behaviors of business researchers and the structure of e-books are perfectly aligned. This structure enables business researchers to quickly locate, identify, and extract specific data. E-books also facilitate business researchers by allowing them overcome the obstacles presented by the fragmented nature of business publishing. For business researchers, all e-books become reference books, enabling them to locate "just the facts." (Simon, 2011, p. 263-264)

3.1.4 *The Literature Review*

The literature review is a summary of scholarly contributions to a field of practice or study that are related and relevant to the topic argued or presented in an author's work; its purpose is to provide evidence from the body of professional literature that shows the scholarly path to and the logical need for that work. This is a pivotal part of the paper in which an author demonstrates his or her case for filling a gap in the literature by addressing its shortcomings, by extending the momentum of previous works, or by correcting the errors of previous works. Simply stated, a thoroughly researched, organized, and well-written literature review effectively sets the stage for the presentation of the subject matter in one's manuscript.

Researching the Literature Review. The purpose of the present text is not to insult the intended readership of LIS professionals by giving instructions on how to conduct database searches. Instead, the purpose is to show that conducting research for a proper literature review is far more involved and sophisticated than rote bibliographic searching. Authors are encouraged to review the following checklist for relevant recommendations.

- **Avoid over-reliance on disciplinary online periodical databases.** Even the most comprehensive databases have significant shortcomings in terms of coverage, indexing, and abstracting.
- **Consult the print literature.** There is considerable depth to the body of literature that precedes the advent and perpetuation of online databases. This source material provides researchers with the instrumental writings of leaders in the field who were contemporary before mass dependence on flawed electronic sources. The use of this material is often an essential ingredient for constructing a strong foundational case for one's own work.
- **Consult the monographic literature.** There is and will continue to be works of great significance to LIS professionals published as books. Although the rules of accessibility are ever-changing, these materials are generally not indexed in or accessible through disciplinary databases. There are many factors in place to guarantee that books will continue as an important component of the professional literature; these include the ongoing profitability of LIS publishing houses, copyright laws that favor publishers, the need for authors to communicate their ideas in book-length works, and the personal reading preferences of researchers that favor the presentation of scholarly content in either print or electronic books.

- **Consult the literature of related disciplines.** There is considerable over-lap in the social sciences, not only in terms of subject matter, but also with applied theory and methodology. Indeed, LIS is a relatively new discipline, and as a result, it borrows much of its relative foundational scholarship from other social sciences. Neglecting this essential material from other disciplines can be a fatal flaw in the literature review.

Organizing the Literature Review. The effective management and organization of research materials retrieved for one's writing project can be challenging, but it is vital part of the literature review process. Although the literature review in a typical library science paper includes citations to and descriptions of one or two dozen other works, the average amount of actual sources retrieved is often two or three times that number. Effectively organizing these research materials helps authors to winnow out only those that are essential to the function of the paper, and to think in a more focused, strategic way about the case they are building in their work. By extension, the quality of organization devoted to supporting research materials also has an impact on the actual writing and ultimate effectiveness of the literature review itself.

Organization begins by focusing on how supporting research materials relate to the main topic of one's work and to the various parts of that main topic. Authors should devise a system of organizing materials that reflects the nature of the subject matter of their manuscript and the manner in which it is presented; this ordinarily involves the establishment of categories. Since the purpose of the literature review is to effectively make the case for one's work, it is generally presented in a logical, sequential manner that reflects those created categories. Although each paper is unique, and necessarily so, some of the more common categories used for organizing research materials include the following:

- **History:** Materials including foundational or fundamental information, disciplinary eras, or chronologies of relevant events
- **Theory:** Materials with theoretical background, direction, or framework
- **Method:** Materials describing the use and effectiveness of methodology, different or similar studies; materials describing qualitative or quantitative methods

- *Discipline:* Materials from LIS or other disciplines
- *Context:* Materials in the context of different library types (e.g., academic, public, school, special), or related professions
- *Source:* Materials by source type (e.g., articles, books, web sites, research instruments, multimedia)
- *Type:* Materials by article type (e.g., bibliographies, case studies, perspectives pieces, research articles, responses, reviews, theoretical works)
- *Author:* Materials by better or lesser known authors
- *Publication:* Materials by impact measures or by perceived levels of prestige
- *Language:* Materials in English or other languages
- *Geography:* Materials by geographic origin (e.g., countries, continents, English-speaking nations, non-English speaking nations)
- *Currency:* Materials by publication date

Bibliographic Management Software. In the contemporary research environment, scholars commonly rely on bibliographic management software to assist with organizing their source materials. These software programs allow users to create or import bibliographic records, to store them in a database for easy retrieval, and to organize them in whichever way they deem to be most useful. The more robust programs allow users to operate on multiple platforms, to store thousands of records, to add and modify research notes, to share data with other citation managers, and to automatically format bibliographic citations and import them into word processing documents. There are dozens of these products available, but Kern and Hensley (2011) assert that the following are currently the most popular:

EndNote (Available: http://www.endnote.com). *EndNote* is a Thomson Reuters product. Institutional subscriptions are available, but most users purchase the program individually. It is a desktop application, which means that users can access their work offline. Online access is available by way of the *EndNote Web* application. Although the web version is commonly used by collaborators from different institutions, it is currently not as powerful as the desktop application. *EndNote* allows users to import records from subscription databases, library catalogs, other citation programs, and web sites. Most major research databases include compatibility features that permit users to import records directly into *EndNote,* but the process is for doing so is different from one database or vendor to another. *EndNote* functions on all major platforms, but in terms of web browsers, there are ongoing problems with *Internet Explorer* and *Safari.* The program allows users to search through the full text of PDF files, and to compare and edit records on the same screen. The program also formats bibliographic citations and allows users to import them into word processing documents.

RefWorks (Available: http://www.refworks.com). *RefWorks* is a Pro-Quest product. Individual subscriptions are available, but most users have access to it by way of an institutional license agreement. It is a web-based program, which means that users can potentially lose access to their work if a license agreement is discontinued. *RefWorks* functions consistently on all major platforms, and it allows users to import records from subscription databases, library catalogs, other citation programs, and web sites. Most major research databases include compatibility features that permit users to import records directly into *RefWorks,* but the process is for doing so is different from one database or vendor to another. Users can currently add up to 100 megabytes of supplementary research materials to their *RefWorks* work space, including most major file types. The program also formats bibliographic citations and allows users to import them into word processing documents.

Zotero (Available: http://www.zotero.org). *Zotero* is product of George Mason University's Center for History and New Media. It is an open source program that comes as a free extension to the *Firefox* web browser. As with other citation managers, *Zotero* allows users to import records from subscription databases, library catalogs, other citation programs, and web sites, but unlike many managers it also captures metadata for PDF and web page files, and it permits searching across them. Most major research databases include compatibility features that permit users to import records directly into *Zotero,* and the simplicity of the program makes for easy learning and using of those features. The program runs conveniently in a separate pane within the browser; users save records to their *Zotero* work space by simply clicking a capture icon, which is located in the web address bar. The icon will change to reflect the type of record to be stored: article, book, image, and so on. An icon appearing as a file folder indicates that multiple items are present on the page displayed. *Zotero* provides cloud service to synchronize data across machines, but it is generally not as robust as *EndNote* or *RefWorks*. The program also formats bibliographic citations and allows users to import them into word processing documents.

As noted above, there are dozens of bibliographic management programs; that number will undoubtedly continue to grow. In the future, researchers will be likely to encounter an increasing number of open access bibliographic management products. The programs described here are currently the most popular, but the relative use and utility of any software program or application is subject to rapid change. Program features will continue to be upgraded, and levels of sophistication will continue to evolve. The purpose of featuring *EndNote*, *RefWorks*, and *Zotero* is simply to show how currently popular programs can be of benefit to authors, particularly during the literature review process.

Writing the Literature Review. Authors must write the literature review in such a way as to build the case for their own work by way of citing and giving credit to previous, related works. This is a standard form of scholarship, and on a larger scale, it is necessary for the cumulative growth of knowledge in a discipline. Beyond simply citing and giving credit to previous works, authors must aptly describe the relevant applications and implications to their own work. Authors must make a convincing case for how previous works are aligned, how they build on one another, and ultimately, how they lead to the main topic that authors have to argue or present in their own papers.

A well-written literature review is another example of form following function; its length and breadth will be dictated by how long it takes and how far afield an author must go to construct a concise, logical argument for the importance of the paper in which it appears. Exhaustive, incomplete, and unfocused presentations of the related literature are among the most common manuscript mistakes. Exhaustive historical accounts of related literature are cumbersome and frustrating to the reader; they bog down the flow and momentum of the argument or case presented. Incomplete accounts fail to provide the strong foundation that is necessary for the argument or case presented to be considered as a useful addition to the literature. Unfocused accounts lead the reader astray and significantly weaken the author's overall argument or presentation.

As with all elements of the scholarly paper, the literature review will differ from one work to another. However, authors are encouraged to review and abide by the following standards, which will apply under most circumstances:

- *Assume that the reader understands the basic premise and subject matter.* Avoid unnecessary and insulting accounts, definitions, descriptions, and histories (e.g., It is unnecessary to define and describe the term "information literacy" in a manuscript intended for the journal, *Communications in Information Literacy*).
- *Cite only those works that are pertinent to the specific subject matter of the manuscript.* Describe only the germane contents of supporting works. Avoid the use of any divergent, general, or peripheral information.
- *Summarize cited works.* Do not over-quote from supporting materials.
- *Show the logic.* Demonstrate the existing connections between cited works and the paper that is being written.
- *Avoid over-citing individual sources.* Readers may regard papers with an over-reliance on particular source materials as derivative.
- *Avoid citing citations.* Be certain to retrieve, read, and cite original sources.
- *Cite primary and secondary sources.* Avoid citing tertiary, unscholarly sources.
- *Cite all attributable statements.* Take care to include proper citations for quotes, paraphrases, and even for general references to scholarly trends.
- *Avoid repetition in descriptions of cited sources.* Avoid manners of expression that are tedious (e.g., "Lavin states that…" "Wells states that…" "Cooper states that…"). Readers will regard overly repetitious accounts of previous works as a lack of author sophistication.

EXAMPLE: Literature Review

Problem-based learning (PBL) is student-directed learning in which the instructor acts as the facilitator and students pursue questions and solutions of their own choosing within the parameters set by the instructor and the project (Bell, 2010). PBL began in medical schools as a result of dramatic and continuing changes in the field. Medical schools found that they were training students for a field in which the knowledge base and skills were evolving so quickly that the content and techniques mastered during medical school were often obsolete by the time the students actually practiced medicine. As a result, some medical schools in the 1960s adopted a PBL approach with its emphasis on the skills necessary to life-long learning. They presented students with simulated patient scenarios of ever increasing complexity. In tackling the problem, students improved their diagnostic and prognostic skills and acquired content along the way (Spence 2004). Necessary to a successful response to the problem is collaboration where together students weigh options, information and outcomes (Savery, 2006). This reflects real world situations which require team work, collaboration, interpersonal skills and the motivation of various team members toward a common goal.

In the last 40 years, PBL has spread well beyond medical instruction. PBL's emphasis on higher-order critical thinking skills, such as understanding and application, proved attractive to teachers of every grade level and across academic disciplines. Studies investigating the effectiveness of PBL indicate that students of this approach acquire better problem solving skills (Bell, 2010; Ravitz, 2009). Moreover, students taught using PBL were more likely than those in more traditional classrooms to report an affinity for the topic of instruction. For example, a study of 270 physics students engaged in self-directed activities reported a more positive attitude towards physics than those students in a teacher-directed class (Erdemir, 2009).

PBL provides a structure for integrating active learning techniques into information literacy instruction; this can often be daunting to librarians faced with limited classroom time and much material to cover (Munro, 2006). As early as 2001, Macklin was describing variations on implementing PBL into information literacy instruction. Building on the use of PBL techniques in medical school, Koufogiannakis et al. (2005), among others, studied the efficacy of taking the PBL teaching technique and extending it into information literacy instruction delivered to medical school students. As PBL-based instruction moved into other disciplinary environments, such as engineering schools, librarians expanded their IL teaching to include PBL instruction for these students. In the context of disciplines that were already heavily invested in PBL instruction, the extension of this technique into the IL environment seemed organic. Studies (Hsieh and Knight, 2008) indicate that engineering students, already familiar with group-centered, task-focused, collaborative technique, find that their research skills also are improved with the use of PBL instruction.

Kenney (2008) provides a framework for using PBL in the traditional "one shot" library session. Using PBL, she argues, benefits all constituents in the information literacy process; students learn more, librarians have more opportunity to engage with students, and classroom faculty members are pleased with the results. Enger et al. (2002) discussed the benefits of incorporating PBL into information literacy sessions and also addressed the challenges inherent with 50 minute one-shot sessions, suggesting that longer sessions and more involvement in the structure of the course would be beneficial. Pelikan (2004) suggests some pragmatic approaches to implementing

EXAMPLE: Literature Review, cont.

PBL in the IL setting. He suggests carefully crafting the flow of the session and preselecting the most helpful and useful resources for students to explore. Snavely (2004) discusses some of the challenges inherent in incorporating PBL techniques in the information literacy setting, including the necessity for more content development and preparation time.

In the context of political science, a problem-based learning approach enhances the push, over the past two decades, to integrate active learning into the political science curriculum. In 1991, John Wahlke, issued a report for the American Political Science Association and the Association of American Colleges in which he identifies purposes in political science education. These include the maximization of "students' capacity to analyze and interpret the significance and dynamics of political events" and the ability "not merely to understand, or to manage their effects . . . but also to evaluate and seek to shape them" (Wahlke, 1991, p.49). Wahlke's report suggests that the mastery of content is empty (or at least diminished) without the acquisition of skills necessary to interpret and synthesize new information.

These critical thinking skills, at their best, serve as a bridge to creative thinking in which the student arrives at conclusions which are uniquely his/her own. Students of politics need not only to interpret and synthesize new information, but also to respond to the dynamic and changing political environment. Kurt Burch (2001) notes how a PBL approach not only promotes the acquisition of skills but also models behavior essential to participatory democracy. The student collaboration, diversity of perspectives, discussion and resolution necessary to the PBL project are the skills necessary to active citizenship. Political science classrooms, at their best, transmit the value of, and excitement in, political participation. Dynamic, engaged political science classrooms open the door between passive and active citizenship; PBL can furnish that door.

So, the PBL emphasis on higher-order critical thinking skills, the increased interest in the subject matter and the stress on collaboration all translate well to a political science classroom. Information literacy is the skill that brings these elements together. A successful, adequate response to the PBL problem requires the ability to distinguish information from misinformation and credible from less credible sources. Alexander (2009) emphasizes the importance of information literacy in a political science context: "I contend that political literacy and information literacy are inextricably linked and impossible to separate" (p. 11).

One of the most useful ways to integrate IL instruction into the political science classroom is to have the IL instruction become a seamless part of the research project process. Cheney (2004) describes a collaborative effort between librarians and faculty at Penn State's School of Information Sciences and Technology. In this process, the librarian and faculty collaborated on creating an assignment for the course that had information literacy goals as intentional steps in the overall research project. Students followed the collaborative PBL model in researching IT-related research questions, and then used what they had found in their class projects. On this basis, Cheney, and others (Spence, 2004) call for more integration of PBL techniques in IL instruction to increase beneficial collaboration between librarians and faculty and also to increase students' abilities to effectively complete college-level research projects.

In summary, PBL effectively brings information literacy and political science together by resisting the separation of subject and process

EXAMPLE: Literature Review, cont.

(Cheney, 2004). PBL demands that students collaborate to respond creatively to a problem; it also requires that faculty and librarians collaborate to generate problems that engage students in an exploration of the subject while acquiring and practicing skills. (Cook & Walsh, 2012, p. 60-62).[1]

The LIS Literature Review. The LIS literature review can differ from other social science literature reviews in an important way: namely, the tense that is used to describe other scholars' works. Although the standard style manuals of the social sciences stipulate that descriptions or discussions of previously published works should be presented in the past tense, it is relatively common and generally accepted for LIS authors to describe and discuss previous works in the present tense. There is a subtle elegance to this particular characteristic; it adds to the notion that all contributing authors, past or present, are part of the ongoing disciplinary discourse. Not all LIS journal editors are accepting of this practice, but most are.

Finally, the literature review is a common element in scholarly LIS papers, but it is not always necessary. Although the scholarly paper requires the author to demonstrate a justification for being published, that does not always need to come by way of a discrete literature review. Some scholarly works may only require a limited number of references to previous works. Authors may include citations to previous works in their introductions, or they may present that information in an interspersed manner throughout the course of a manuscript. Journals rarely have specific rules for the construction of literature reviews, but they always have editorial preferences. Authors are encouraged to review multiple issues of the journals they are considering to assess those preferences.

3.1.5 *The Method*

Scholarly LIS journal literature includes a high percentage of research articles, or case studies that involve an element of research to assess the effectiveness of the cases presented. For these works it is often necessary to include a method section. The purpose of the method section is to provide a complete description of how a study was conducted, allowing readers to see how the results were generated, and also to judge the validity and reliability of those results. Additionally, the method section will include any operational definitions; these are provided so readers can understand all the dynamics and variables of the study. Ultimately, the well-written method section provides the necessary directions for other LIS professionals to replicate the study for the purposes of their own research or for the benefit of their own institutions.

In the instance of research-intensive papers, authors may need to subdivide the method section and provide separate, detailed descriptions of participants or subjects, sample sizes, procedures for selecting subjects or participants, operational definitions, measurement instruments, research designs, or any manipulations or intervening circumstances that might have an impact on the study. For ongoing or replicated studies, the details of which were previously published, authors may simply cite the original source, offer a functional summary, and then detail any necessary modifications.

EXAMPLE: Replicated Study

The methods Kohl and Davis used in the original study were replicated with an expanded set of journal titles... (Nisonger & Davis, 2005, p. 343)

The key to an effectively written method section is clarity, and if at all possible, brevity. Authors are encouraged to review and abide by the following standards:

- **Provide the context** of the study, but avoid trivial, unrelated details (e.g., It may be necessary to indicate that a study was conducted in an academic library, but it may not be necessary to divulge that it is in a public, doctoral-granting university, located in the southeastern United States, consisting of 11,000 graduate students, 17,000 undergraduate students, 20 doctoral programs, et cetera).
- **Describe the methodology** of the study (e.g., Indicate how the study was conducted, what results were collected, how were results analyzed).
- **Describe the participants** or subjects in the study, but avoid trivial, unrelated details (e.g., It may be necessary to indicate that study participants were undergraduate psychology students between the ages of 18 and 21 years old, but it may not be necessary to give a breakdown their gender, race, socioeconomic status, et cetera).
- **Specify the size of the sample** used in the study, and describe the how participants or subjects were selected (e.g., "Two hundred thirty-four instruction librarians from North American college or university libraries, who were solicited by way of the Information Literacy Instruction Discussion List, and who volunteered to participate...").
- **Describe the instruments used** to generate results (e.g., examination results, independent course evaluation, focus group, interview, questionnaire, survey, et cetera).
- **Define operational variables** (e.g., Define dependent variables, independent variables, relevant theory, specific measurements, et cetera).
- **Include intervening circumstances** (e.g., possible limitations, uncontrolled variables, unanticipated variables, et cetera).
- **Use the past tense.** Even when research is ongoing, the manuscript will report on events in the past and on completed work.
- **Avoid listing results.** The purpose of the method section is to describe how a study was conducted. Study results are reserved for the results section of the paper.

EXAMPLE: Method Section

This study employed a syllabus methodology to examine the research tasks required of first-semester, first-year students at a large university in the southeastern United States that admits approximately 4,000 new students per year.

A random sample of 350 first-semester, first-year students was obtained from the university registrar, a sample size large enough to make inferences to the population of first-year students at the university. The information provided for each student included the sections and courses in which the student was enrolled. This information was entered into a relational database for analysis. Then, the syllabi and available assignment descriptions for each student were collected via course Web sites or through instructor contacts. Because not all instructors responded to the researchers' request for information, syllabi for every course could not be obtained. In fact, complete course information was collected for only 139 students. Next, the course information for all 350 students was carefully examined. If class assignments did not require students to complete any research tasks, a value of "n" was entered into the database. When class assignments required completion of a research task, a value of "yes" was entered and the assignments were analyzed to determine which broad types of research tasks were required.

Because CII programs are skill-based approaches to instruction, librarians who develop them need to know what skills students are required to demonstrate to complete their assignments. As a result, the categories used in this study focus on the outcomes students are required to demonstrate through the completion of tasks, rather than

> **EXAMPLE: Method Section, cont.**
>
> the amount of library use or the assignment outputs (such as a "research paper" or "annotated bibliography"). The broad categories of outcomes were: 1) find Web sites; 2) find articles; 3) find books; 4) find reference books; and 5) find data and statistics. At first glance, these outcome categories appear to be focused on Standard 2 of the Information Literacy Competency Standards for Higher Education, "The information literate student accesses needed information effectively and efficiently." However, each outcome category includes skills associated with other Standards. For example, students required to "find articles" must be able to recognize the need for an article, select a database, construct a search, evaluate results, locate a print or online copy, and cite the article -- skills that can be mapped to multiple Standards. (VanScoy & Oakleaf, 2008, p. 569-570)

Scholarly LIS journals rarely have specific rules for the construction of method sections. However, editorial expectations are standard across the discipline in terms of clarity, brevity, elements to include, and elements to avoid. Authors are encouraged to review multiple issues of the journals they are considering to assess more subtle editorial preferences. Authors seeking assistance with research methodology are highly encouraged to consult Beck and Manuel's (2004) authoritative text on the topic, *Practical Research Methods for Librarians and Information Professionals*.

3.1.6 *The Results*

The results section of a scholarly paper includes a summary of study findings—whether quantitative or qualitative—and an analysis of those findings relevant to the hypothesis presented in the introduction and to the interpretation presented in the discussion section. A relevant and focused results section is critical. The presentation of too much information, or the inclusion of information that is not pertinent to the main topic, dilutes the author's argument. Conversely, the omission of unexpected findings, or those that run counter to the hypothesis, corrupts the integrity of the author's work. Authors must be disciplined about presenting all the relevant results, but just the relevant results.

The results section should be constructed in a logical fashion that follows the path of the main argument in the paper and parallels the construction of other sections. It is a common mistake for authors to build or organize this section based the chronological order of discovery in the study. It is also a common mistake for authors to include discussion of methodology in this section, which is repetitive and sloppy, and by extension, weakens the author's overall argument. As with the method section, authors should remember that published papers report on past events; as such, the results section should be written in the past tense.

Based on the subject matter of the manuscript and on the nature of the argument or presentation, authors will sometimes find it necessary to subdivide the results section. This is very common in scholarly LIS journal articles; it is done to parse out discrete findings, and also to bolster important parts of an author's main argument. When subdivision is necessary, authors should use brief, but appropriately descriptive subheadings to assist the reader. Based on the subject matter of the manuscript and on the nature of the argument or presentation, authors may also find it necessary to combine the results and discussion sections. This, too, is common in LIS journal articles. In this instance, the combined section can be expanded to accommodate the necessary analysis and discussion. Otherwise, the results section should be brief, concise, and driven solely by the findings.

Figures. The results section of the paper often includes the use of figures. These can be charts, diagrams, illustrations, images, and screen captures, but in the context of the scholarly paper, they are most commonly graphs and tables. Figures are used to demonstrate a study's overall results in an easily comprehensible manner, and also to facilitate the reader's understanding of specific results that are relevant to the discussion section, which follows. The following standards apply to the use of figures in scholarly papers:

- **Follow the guidelines.** Most scholarly LIS journals have specific rules for the construction and use of figures, including font, length, and placement within the manuscript.

> **EXAMPLE: Author Guidelines for Figures**
>
> Tables and figures (illustrations) should not be embedded in the text, but should be included as separate sheets or files. A short descriptive title should appear above each table with a clear legend and any footnotes suitably identified below. All units must be included. Figures should be completely labeled, taking into account necessary size reduction. Captions should be typed, double-spaced, on a separate sheet. (Taylor & Francis, 2012, para. 8)

- **Be professional.** A poorly designed figure defeats its own purpose.
- **Be simple.** Avoid lengthy or overly descriptive figures; use only the necessary space and text. Figures are intended to provide the reader with a quick and easy-to-understand representation of study results. Avoid the use of anything that detracts from the primary purpose of a figure.
- **Present condensed, rich information.** Figures should be used to represent information that is difficult to articulate or to grasp in the form of prose. Avoid the use of figures to represent information that is more appropriately articulated and better understood in one or in a few sentences of prose.
- **Avoid gratuitous use.** Do not repeat information that is presented in other figures, and do not use figures simply for the sake of using figures.

Block Quotes. The results section is also an appropriate area of the paper to highlight selected portions of collected data; this is done for the purpose of bolstering the author's hypothesis, exemplifying particular data sets, or representing overall findings. Most often this is done by inserting targeted block quotes from study participants into relevant areas of the results section. As with the use of figures, however, authors must take care to avoid gratuitous or unnecessary block quotes; they should be used only for the purposes noted above.

EXAMPLE: [from] Results Section

Results of the number of students per librarians are presented in Figure 1. Of the campuses surveyed in our study, four-year private institutions averaged 318 students per librarian in 2009 and 376 students per librarian in 2011. Four-year public institutions averaged 696 students per librarian in 2009 and 637 students per librarian in 2011. Two-year public institutions averaged 932 students per librarian in 2009 and 1094 students per librarian in 2011.

On average, four-year private institutions do have a lower student-to-librarian ratio than four-year public institutions. Also, both four-year (public and private) have a lower student-to-librarian ratio than the two-year colleges. Several of these data points are of note as they are potentially misleading. It appears from the data we studied that the average number of students per librarian dropped by 59 at public, four-year institutions from 2009 to 2011. Unfortunately, though, this is likely not the case. Several new institutions were added to the distribution list for the 2011 survey, at least one of which had a very low student-to-librarian ratio. This skewed the results.

Also of note is the increase in the average number of students per librarian at two-year, public institutions. On first glance, one may assume that these institutions must have downsized their staffs to

EXAMPLE: [from] Results Section, cont.

account for this rapid increase. To the best of our knowledge, that has not been the case. Rather, the rapid increase in their student-to-librarian ratios is better explained by the implementation of Arkansas's state-wide lottery scholarship program. The program provides scholarship money to many students who might not otherwise be able to attend school. Because of that, enrollment at many schools has increased, thereby raising the student-per-librarian ratio.

Figure 1: **The averages were calculated from the FTE and number of librarians. Numbers represent actual number of students per one librarian: 182 librarians in 2009 and 194 librarians in 2011**

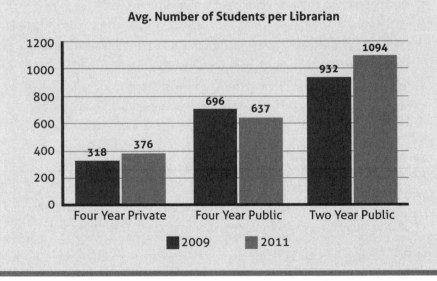

Avg. Number of Students per Librarian

Scholarly LIS journals rarely have specific rules for the overall construction of method sections; editorial expectations are standard across the discipline in terms of clarity, brevity, elements to include, and elements to avoid. Still, authors are encouraged to review multiple issues of the journals they are considering to assess more subtle editorial preferences, particularly in terms of length, use of subheadings, use of figures, and the potential for combined results and discussion sections.

3.1.7 *The Discussion*

The discussion section is the part of the scholarly paper in which authors effectively use evidence presented in the results section to make their argument. If the results are properly presented, then authors will be well positioned to evaluate and interpret them relative to the original hypothesis. The discussion section is where authors interpret results, draw conclusions, and assert the implications relative to the main topic of the paper. Given that the discipline of library and information science is based primary in professional practice, the implications will usually be of a functional or practical nature. However, it is also important for authors to apply any relevant theoretical implications. This can be a difficult section of the paper to write, but for the purposes of getting published and making a noteworthy contribution to the literature, it is essentially the most important.

A significant percentage of the LIS journal literature is presented in the form of case studies, perspectives pieces, and theoretical articles (see Types of Articles section). Elements of these types of works do not always align perfectly with the prescribed format for presenting scholarly social science papers; this is particularly true for the effective use of discussion sections. It is generally understood that the aforementioned types of articles do not always make use of evidence in the same way that most social science papers do. It is also true, however, that many LIS papers lack the substance that necessitates the use of discussion sections. Contemporary LIS literature has an unhealthy number of authors who do not understand the process of presenting an argument by way of the scholarly paper, and the vital role that the discussion section plays in the ultimate success or failure of that argument. Authors are highly encouraged to abide by the following rules for constructing a proper discussion section in their manuscript:

- **Begin with an unambiguous statement in support or in nonsupport of the original hypothesis.** Do not clutter the beginning of the results section with unclear language, and do not conflate it with information already provided in previous sections.

EXAMPLE: Support or Nonsupport of Hypothesis

The present study investigated how the presence and timing of domain information influences scientific reasoning and knowledge acquisition in low prior knowledge students. Presenting domain information per se was predicted to enhance hypothesis-driven inquiry and knowledge acquisition. Presenting domain information at the right time (i.e., before as well as during the inquiry) was further expected to yield similar advantages over a situation where domain information is merely available before the inquiry. Both hypotheses were supported by the results. (Lazonder, Hagemans, & de Jong, 2010, p. 518).

As framed by our research questions, this study sheds more light on the extent and reasons for the late hiring of teachers, especially in large urban school districts. (Loubert & Nelson, 2010, p. 437)

- **Use parallel construction.** The discussion section should follow the logical path of an author's argument or presentation, and the construction of it should follow the order and organization of the results section.
- **Specify the implications** in terms of theory and professional practice, but avoid over-claiming correlative relationships as causal ones.
- **Indicate the significance.** Complete the argument or presentation by telling the reader what the results show. Be explicit in terms of the importance and noteworthiness of the work, but take care not to dramatize or to overstate.

EXAMPLE: Indicate the Significance

This study has important contributions to higher education literature. It fills an important gap in the higher education institutions' service quality literature by proposing the LibZOT model for library services. The proposed model can be effectively used as a diagnostic tool in the higher education sector to improve quality of library services that have significant effect on overall student satisfaction. (Nadiri & Mayboudi, 2010, p. 15)

- *Be critical.* Discuss the level of certainty related to the results and implications. Thoroughly vet the possible alternatives, anomalies, or contradictions.
- *Discuss limitations.* Acknowledge any imprecisions, intervening factors, or shortcomings, but do not be apologetic for them. These are the realities of social science research. Use the limitations as leverage for suggesting future research.

EXAMPLE: Discuss Limitations

Primarily, because this study is done from the literature without the interviews, visits and observations of primary sources, this study presents inherent weaknesses. However, this type of study may be considered an exploratory study for a further study of curricula by graduate library schools. New hypotheses discovered in this data may provide bases for future research. This type of research should help evolve a new depth of esprit de corps between profession library education in Cataloging and Classification and professional librarianship in these and related areas. (McAllister-Harper, 1993, p. 105)

- **Relate to previous works.** Show how the presented work confirms or contradicts previous research, and discuss the possible reasons why.

EXAMPLE: Relate to Previous Works

The results of this study confirm many of the conclusions of previous studies investigating Latinos' perceptions of libraries. Solis and Dabbour and Whitmire suggested that Latino students use the library less frequently, seek assistance from librarians less often, and demonstrate lower levels of information literacy than students of other racial and ethnic groups. While the principal investigator cannot conclude how the participants in this study compare against students of other racial and ethnic groups, the results indicate that these Latino students do, in fact, use the library relatively late in their academic experience and arguably do not utilize the library's resources to their full advantage. (Long, 2011, p. 510)

- **Avoid repetition.** Repeating information from the results section is a common mistake in scholarly papers. Unless the results and discussion sections are combined, the latter should be devoted to discussing, but not repeating the former.
- **Avoid meandering.** Provide thoughtful, but concise discussion of the results. Do not stray from the established order and organization, and do not keep the reader in the discussion section any longer than is absolutely necessary.

Based on the subject matter of the manuscript and on the nature of one's argument or presentation, authors will sometimes find it necessary to subdivide the discussion section. Typically this is done to mirror the organization of the results section, and it is common a practice in scholarly LIS journal articles. As with subdivision of the results section, it is done to parse out discrete elements in an author's main argument. When subdivision is necessary, authors should use brief, but appropriately descriptive sub-headings to assist the reader. It is also a common practice in LIS litera-ture to label this section of the scholarly paper "analysis," "implications," or something else that is relevant to the main topic and the type of paper. Authors may even forego the discussion section altogether, but this prac-tice is discouraged. Ultimately, these issues are resolved by way of review and editorial processes.

Scholarly LIS journals rarely have specific rules for the construction of discussion sections, but editorial expectations are standard across the dis-cipline in terms of clarity, brevity, elements to include, and elements to avoid. Still, authors are encouraged to review multiple issues of the jour-nals they are considering to assess more subtle editorial preferences, par-ticularly in terms of length, use of subheadings, and the potential use of combined sections.

3.1.8 The Conclusion

It is somewhat common for the discussion to be the final section of schol-arly papers in the social sciences. However, it is far more common in LIS papers to finish with a separate, concluding section. An effective conclu-sion provides a summary of the paper's main argument and significance. Consequently, this section of the paper should contain no revelations or inherent surprises to the reader. As Henry and Roseberry (1997) described, "The term 'conclusion' is taken from the point at which the writer stops explaining or defending the proposition to the end of the text" (p. 483). To make a legal comparison, this is the author's concluding argument. It is incumbent on the author to conclude by stating the relevance and signifi-cance of the paper relative to the main topic, to the broader context of the literature, and even to one's discipline or professional practice. This must be done in a fresh, powerful, and resonant manner that does not simply repeat language from earlier sections of the manuscript.

The conclusion is an appropriate area of the paper for authors to reaf-firm an argument, to reassert implications, to suggest future research direc-tions, and even to offer personal insights. Still, brevity and concision are paramount. Save for the abstract, the conclusion is most often the shortest section of the scholarly LIS paper.

EXAMPLE: Conclusion

As with any assessment, in addition to sharing the findings in the literature, these findings are now guiding our library's online video tutorial revision and continued development. In addition to editing the existing video, the best practices identified will be incorporated into the internal guidelines for developing video tutorials. That students were not aware of the availability of the tutorials is a concern, and efforts will be made to work with the website advisory committee to better integrate the tutorials throughout the library's website as well as to collaborate with the virtual reference training coordinators to encourage referrals to the tutorials at teachable moments during a chat reference session. Incorporating the videos into the institution's digital repository may also assist with findability and raised awareness of their availability. Finally, for those times when the Ask-a-Librarian service is not available, a more prominent link to the tutorials might provide an alternate form of assistance for patrons with basic questions.

Future research on online video tutorials is needed as this study only begins to lay out the best practices related to instructional effectiveness. Such a study would be akin to that conducted by Lindsay, Cummings, Johnson, and Scales (2007) for more traditional web-based tools. Such a large scale study with students who do not know how to complete certain tasks, which are taught through video tutorials followed by performance-based assessments, would give great insight into how well videos can be used to teach and whether their effectiveness is restricted to students with particular learning styles and/or specific content, for example, procedural, rather than conceptual. (Bowles-Terry, Hensley, & Hinchliffe, 2010, p. 27)

3.1.9 *The References*

The intended audience of LIS professionals knows very well the purpose and importance of references: to acknowledge the works that are cited in the body of the manuscript, and to provide reliable information for retrieving those works. All scholarly journals require their authors to abide by a standard style of documenting references. Chicago Style, as set forth in the *Chicago Manual of Style*, is most commonly used in LIS literature. American Psychological Association (APA) Style, as set forth in the *Publication Manual of the American Psychological Association*, is increasingly popular in the discipline, particularly with electronic-only journals. Some LIS journals or publishers require the use of other formats. As an example, Emerald requires prospective authors to use Harvard Style for documenting references in their LIS publications. As a general rule, however, the Chicago and APA Styles are the standards of the discipline. Such requirements will be expressly stated on a journal's web site, or in the front or back matter of its print edition.

3.1.10 *The Appendices*

Appendices are supplemental materials to the scholarly paper; they are not essential, but they serve to clarify, explain, or expound on elements of the main topic. Generally, these materials are considered to be too distracting, too long, or too unwieldy for inclusion in the body of the text, but they are helpful for readers who seek additional information on the main topic. The types of articles most commonly published in LIS journals—case studies and research papers—often require the use of appendices. Examples include data collection instruments (e.g., assessments, survey questionnaires, and tests), figures (e.g., charts, graphs, illustrations, images, screen captures, and tables), lists, or other relevant documents. Electronic journals may also include sound and video recordings as appendices.

With print journals, appendices are positioned after the references. With electronic journals, appendices are either positioned after the references, or they are linked to from an appropriate area of the article or the journal's web site. Scholarly LIS journals rarely have specific rules for the addition, construction, content, and presentation of appendices; editorial decisions on supplemental materials are generally based on what is reasonable to include and what is relevant to the main topic. Authors should abide by the rules for appendices that are included the required manuals of style for the journals they are considering.

4

Elements of Selecting the Right Journal

Selecting the appropriate journal for one's scholarly work seems like an obvious step in the publishing process, but elements of this are sometimes dismissed, overlooked, or even misunderstood. As with practitioners, scholars, and theorists in other disciplines, LIS professionals are generally familiar with the body of literature that is relevant to their specific interests. However, just as a thorough literature review is necessary for exploring gaps in professional discourse, and for setting the stage in one's own writing, a highly methodical bibliographic review is necessary for identifying appropriate journals for one's work.

The discipline and practice of library and information science (LIS) is ever-evolving, and as a natural result, so, too, is the professional literature. New journals emerge (e.g., *Collaborative Librarianship*, 2009-present), and some are discontinued (e.g., *Research Strategies*, 1983-2005). Changes are driven by ongoing developments in LIS, the ever-increasing quantity of scholarly output, technological advances, the economics of scholarly communication, the momentum of the free web, and even by changeovers in editorship and evolutions in editorial philosophies. The importance of fully researching and then selecting the journals that are currently appropriate for one's work cannot be overstated.

Elements to Consider. The general subject matter and the more defined scope of a publication should be examined first. The publication type needs be determined: Is it a scholarly journal or a trade publication? If it is the former, which is the purview of this text, authors need to consider the preferred type of articles published in a journal—bibliographies, case studies, perspectives pieces, research articles, responses, reviews, or theoretical works. The target audience is critical; although different publications may be dedicated to the same subject area, each one is likely to be intended for professionals in a specific type of institution, in a specialized context, and sometimes even in a select geographic region. Prospective authors might find it necessary to investigate a journal's prestige within the profession, its rankings when compared to other disciplinary publications (e.g., impact factor, Eigenfactor score, H-index), and its strengths and weaknesses in terms of medium, indexing, and dissemination. It is often worthwhile to inspect a journal's publisher, its publication history and schedule, its reputation, and even the composition of its editorial board. Authors are also encouraged to investigate practical matters such as a journal's acceptance rates, response times, submission and review processes, and writing style. All these aspects are discussed in this chapter.

Subject Area and Scope

Given the nature of their work, librarians are generally more skilled than professionals in other disciplines at researching appropriate outlets for their scholarly writing. One should begin by identifying those journals most that are fitting in terms of general subject area, and then by determining the particular specializations of those publications. Each academic journal has a scope that is its scholarly niche, and as a result each publication has a specific and well-defined readership.

Since the discipline of LIS is based primarily in professional practice, significant numbers of its scholarly journals are functional in nature. That is, many of the discipline's journals are dedicated to functional areas of librarianship (e.g., *Reference & User Services Quarterly*; *Library Collections, Acquisitions, & Technical Services*; *Journal of Interlibrary Loan, Document Delivery & Information Supply*). The scope of some LIS journals can also be broad in nature, covering multiple areas of professional practice, but those same publications may be dedicated specifically to current research, case studies, or recent developments (e.g., *Library Trends*; *portal: Libraries and the Academy*; *Journal of Library Innovation*).

The purview of a journal may involve a specific to a type of library (e.g., *Community & Junior College Libraries*; *Notes*; *Public Libraries*; *Law Library Journal*), or perhaps an individual institution and its collections (e.g., *Harvard Library Bulletin*; *Princeton University Library Chronicle*). A journal may be dedicated to professional education (e.g., *Journal of Education for Library and Information Science*), to the works of graduate students (e.g., *Current Studies in Librarianship*), or to the presentation of professional research (e.g., *College & Research Libraries*; *Library Quarterly*). The scope may also be regional (e.g., *Colorado Libraries*), national (e.g., *Canadian Journal of Information and Library Science*), or international (e.g., *International Journal of Knowledge Management*).

Importantly, an academic journal will always have multiple layers comprising its scope. As an example, the *Journal of Academic Librarianship* (JAL) presents research findings, case studies, and other types of scholarly papers on all areas of academic librarianship, and its contributors and readership are international. Although JAL is widely considered to be a prestigious publication, its scope is a broad one. Conversely, the *Journal of the Library Administration and Management Section* presents academic papers limited to the subject area of library management for different types of libraries, and its contributors and readership are members of the New York Library Association. Clearly, this is a narrower scope, but it defines the journal, and it demonstrates the ultimate point that prospective authors must do their research in terms of finding the appropriate outlet for their scholarship. The paragraphs below provide standard sources to consult and best practices to follow.

Ulrichsweb: Global Serials Directory (Available: http://www.ulrichsweb .com). Formerly titled *Ulrich's International Periodicals Directory*, this subscription-based directory provides bibliographic information for over 300,000 periodicals, including more than 650 active, scholarly, English language LIS journals.[1] Records for each journal include useful information for prospective authors: status, publisher, content type, scope note, format, publication frequency, editor name(s) and contact information, readership demographics, abstracting and indexing, and even professional reviews. *Ulrichsweb* does not easily allow for searching by way of fine-grained subject headings; instead, users must use a combination of skillfully crafted search strategies and advanced search features or limiters. For this reason, it is often necessary to execute numerous searches in an effort to be thorough.

WorldCat (Available: http://newfirstsearch.oclc.org). Commonly referred to as the world's largest library catalog, *WorldCat* is a subscription-based bibliographic database that includes over 100 million records contributed by more than 20,000 libraries worldwide.[2] The advantage of using this source for identifying appropriate journals is the ability to search by fine-grained subject headings (e.g., Medicine – Library resources – Periodicals). Records for each journal include status, publisher, content type, format, publication frequency, names and numbers of subscribing institutions, and sometimes the editor name(s) and contact information. Records do not include all-important readership demographics, scope notes, or indexing and abstracting information. There is a free web version of *WorldCat* (available at http://www.worldcat.org), but it is generally less robust and less functional than the full, subscription-based version.

Journal Databases. The purpose of the present text is not to insult the intended audience of LIS professionals by giving instructions on how to conduct database searches. Instead, the purpose is to offer some important recommendations and reminders. To be certain, LIS databases are necessary sources for reviewing the literature, but they are also valuable tools for determining where relevant subject matter is currently being published. Currently, the premier databases for this type of research are *Library Literature & Information Science Full Text, Library, Information Science & Technology Abstracts with Full Text* (*LISTA*), *Library & Information Science Source*, and *Library and Information Science Abstracts* (*LISA*). The standard education databases provide some overlapping, but sometimes complementary coverage of library literature; these sources include *Education Resources Information Center* (*ERIC*), *Education Research Complete, Education Full Text*, and *Education Source*. Multidisciplinary databases, like *Academic Search Complete* and *Academic OneFile*, also provide overlapping and complementary coverage, but with far less depth or focus.

Subject librarians and departmental liaisons would do well to consult the literature of the other academic or professional disciplines that they serve, and to consider publishing there as well. As an example for the myriad subject librarians with teaching responsibilities, most disciplines have journals that are devoted to pedagogy in their field, and all of them have journals that welcome well-crafted and unique case studies on effective, instruction librarian-faculty partnerships. A list of discipline-specific journals is maintained by the Association of College and Research Libraries on their Selective List of Journals on Teaching & Learning web site (2013).

The significance of currency cannot be overstated when using databases to find appropriate journals. As noted above, the scopes and foci of journals are ever-changing; so, too, is the professional vernacular of library science. As LIS professionals, the intended readers of this text are accustomed to and skilled at using subject headings when searching databases. However, the indexers, abstracters, linguists, and programmers employed by database vendors are generally slow to react to changes in the profession. As a result, the use of descriptors and subject headings often fail to produce the most current and relevant search results. Consider, as an example, the relatively recent evolution of LIS vernacular from "library orientation" to "bibliographic instruction," to "library instruction," to "information literacy instruction." Although professionals rarely use the term "library orientation" today, the thesaurus in the *Library & Information Science Full Text* database still directs users to that heading.[3] Prospective authors should employ a combination of controlled vocabulary and free text search strategies in order to generate the most current and relevant results.

Cabell's Directory of Publishing Opportunities in Educational Technology and Library Science (Available: http://www.cabells.com). This subscription-based directory provides useful information for LIS researchers and academics seeking to match their work with appropriate scholarly journals. The directory indexes 220 titles, and for each one it includes journal contact information, publication history and frequency, descriptive subject terms, targeted audience, manuscript guidelines, review processes and response times, and when available, acceptance rates.[4] As with most directories, this one is easy to navigate, and the information is presented in a standardized and uncluttered manner. The subject coverage provided in each journal profile is presented as topical keywords; this is somewhat helpful to users, but the directory does not include more descriptive scope notes. Moreover, this directory does not constitute a comprehensive or focused listing of LIS journal titles; publications from other, somewhat tertiary research and practitioner areas, such as distance education and telecommunications, are also included.

LIS Publications Wiki (Available: http://slisapps.sjsu.edu/wikis/faculty/putnam/index.php/Main_Page). The *LIS Publications Wiki* was created in 2007 by Laurie Putnam from San José State University's School of Library and Information Science. Specifically, the site was developed as a service learning exercise for students in Putnam's "Publishing for the Profession" class. *LIS Publications Wiki* is a free web source that provides relevant and practical information on LIS the publishing universe—scholarly journals, trade periodicals, books, and online forums—for prospective authors. Apropos of this text, the scholarly journals section currently includes profiles for only 60 titles. [5] Profiles are contributed mainly by Putnam's students, but the community of LIS editors, publishers, and other professionals are also invited to participate. As a matter of their "Publishing for the Profession" course assignment, student contributors are instructed to contact the editors of journals that they profile, and to encourage necessary corrections and revisions.

Each *LIS Publications Wiki* entry includes a description of the journal, including scope, target audience, publisher, medium, content, publication schedule, indexing and dissemination, contact information, submission guidelines, response times, and when the information is available, acceptance rates. Entries also include a readership analysis and an evaluation of each title's potential impact for authors; the latter of these can come across as subjective, but the wiki platform allows for easy and open editorial revisions. Currently, the *LIS Publications Wiki* has a queue of several unclaimed scholarly journal titles awaiting analysis and evaluation from Putnam's students and other contributing professionals. [6]

Free Web. No rational librarian can dispute the fact that the free web is becoming an increasingly relevant and important tool for conducting research. This is also true for finding journals that are appropriate for one's scholarly work. Anecdotal evidence of this is provided by one of academic librarianship's preeminent voices, Barbara Fister (2007), in her foreword to the first print edition of the open access journal, *Communications in Information Literacy*:

> I was burrowing around the Web one day, looking for useful ideas on faculty/librarian collaboration, and bumped into a remarkable article by Claire McGuinness in which she challenges the usual one-faculty-one-member-at-a-time approach and argues for institution-wide integration of information literacy. Perfect! Even better, it appeared in an issue of a journal that included interesting articles from three countries— all of them practical, thoughtful, carefully written and well-documented—and all of them about information literacy. I had struck gold. (p. *i*)

The majority of today's scholarly publishers have a web presence, which allow for live data to be collected by external systems on the free web. *Google Scholar* (available at http://scholar.google.com/) is a presently the most valuable web tool for finding scholarly source materials that may or may not turn up in traditional or subscription-based indexes, directories, and databases. As with journal databases, *Google Scholar* generates results based on relevance, available metadata, bibliographic information, and provided text. The proprietary nature of most published materials may preclude full text access for records that appear in search results. Still, *Google Scholar* serves as a free web index, a partially full text database, and a targeted search engine all at once, and that makes for a powerful research tool. A possible emerging alternative for free web bibliographic searching is *Microsoft Academic Search* (available at http://academic.research.microsoft.com/), but to date there are no compelling studies suggesting significant advantages of using it over *Google Scholar*. Authors are also recommended to consult the *Directory of Open Access Journals* (DOAJ) to look for suitable LIS publications (see Open Access section).

4.1 Types of Journals

Non-Academic Periodicals

The greater body of LIS literature includes a variety of serial publication types, including newsletters, trade magazines, proceedings, and scholarly journals. The primary focus of this text is to serve as a guide for LIS authors who intend to publish in scholarly journals, with an emphasis on peer-reviewed publications. However, for the purpose of assisting prospective authors to identify and distinguish between types of serials, the following are common, non-academic periodicals existing in LIS literature:

Newsletters. Newsletters publish short, informal articles on a wide range of popular topics for LIS professionals. These are cheaply produced publications, usually without commercial advertisements, and most often published by professional associations, or by divisions or committees from within those associations. Most newsletters have adopted an electronic distribution model, usually by way of membership discussion lists. They are typi-cally regional in scope, or targeted to a broader audience of professionals in a particular specialty area of librarianship. Articles in these publications do not include substantive discussions or presentations of scholarly subject matter, and they rarely contain in-depth analyses or citations to other works. Although they serve a useful purpose for their audiences, little weight is given by hiring, promotion, or tenure review committees to articles pub-lished in newsletters. Examples of these publications include *Instruction Section Newsletter* (ACRL), *American Indian Library Association Newsletter*, and *Association of Law Libraries of Upstate New York Newsletter*.

Trade Magazines. Alternatively known as professional journals, these peri-odicals publish relatively short, informal articles on a wide range of popu-lar topics for LIS professionals. They can be regional in scope, or targeted to a broader audience of professionals in specific types of libraries. As with newsletters, articles in these publications do not include substantive discussions or presentations of scholarly subject matter, and they rarely contain in-depth analyses or citations to other works. Unlike newsletters, trade magazines usually include upscale, commercial advertisements, and they are generally of a high production quality. Still, little weight is given by hiring, promotion, or tenure review committees to articles pub-lished in trade magazines. Examples of these publications include *Ameri-can Libraries*, *Ohio Libraries*, *School Library Journal*, and *College & Research Libraries News*.

Proceedings. Proceedings are periodicals that include papers presented at professional association, professional institute, or professional society conferences. They are commonly published on an annual or biannual basis under the same title, but they are sometimes published as parts of a mono-graphic series with unique titles. Although papers presented at conferences are often competitively selected, those same works published in proceedings periodicals are generally not considered to be peer-reviewed. Occasion-ally, peer-reviewed LIS journals will publish proceedings papers in theme issues, or in those that are devoted entirely to the coverage of a particu-lar conference. As an example, *Reference Services Review* devotes biannual, special issues to papers presented at LOEX-of-the-West conference. How-ever, papers included in these special issues are generally not considered to be peer-reviewed, and published proceedings do not always include all the presented papers of professional conferences. Furthermore, authors cannot simply submit their works to be considered for these publications; inclusion is by invitation and presentation only.

The perceived impact or significance of papers published in proceedings periodicals varies from institution to institution, and from area to area within LIS. Proceedings papers are given much greater weight in the information science community than in the library science community, and they are typically published as monographic serials. As a general rule, however, these works are not regarded as highly as those that undergo the formal review process. Examples of these serial publications include *ARL Proceedings of the Meetings, Computers in Libraries [Year] Conference Proceedings, Association of Jewish Libraries: Proceedings of the Annual Convention,* and *Proceedings of the [Number] Text Retrieval Conference.*

Professional Weblogs. Colloquially referred to as blogs, professional weblogs are free, web-based serial publications that are developed and maintained by professional LIS associations. Most associations have their own weblogs and official staff bloggers, but most also solicit for relevant content from their broader membership communities. Weblogs are essentially web-based bulletins or communiques; their purpose is not scholarly, although that may change as the nature of scholarly communication is forced to adapt to new publication models. It is also worth noting that countless weblogs are developed and maintained independently by individual LIS professionals, and that some of those publications are highly respectable in terms of content and production quality. However, there is no question that, at present, little weight is given to weblogs by hiring, promotion, or tenure review committees.

Scholarly (Peer-Reviewed) Journals

Scholarly journals are comprised of lengthy, formally prepared articles on refined subject matter that is particular to the scope of each individual publication. These periodicals are intended for highly specified audiences of LIS practitioners, researchers, and specialists. Articles in these journals are written in a prescribed formal style, and in an academic vernacular that is that is understandable to those highly specified audiences. Such articles include substantive arguments or presentations of scholarly subject matter, and they contain in-depth analyses and citations to other relevant works. Scholarly journals are typically of high production quality, and they are produced by commercial, academic, or professional association publishers.

In the greater body of LIS literature, scholarly journals are almost always peer-reviewed—a descriptive term that is synonymous with refereed and juried. All of these terms refer to the same process by which manuscripts are submitted to a scholarly journal, and then distributed to a number of subject experts for professional evaluation and commentary. The subject experts, who are peers in the profession or in a particular field of study, serve as manuscript reviewers, referees, and jurors; thus the terms peer-reviewed, refereed, and juried. Critical to the integrity of this process, information that might potentially identify reviewers or individual authors and their institutions is removed from submitted manuscripts prior to review; thus the related term "blind-reviewed" (see Peer Review section).

As noted, there are currently more than 650 active, scholarly, English language LIS journals; they represent every area of the academic discipline and every specialty of professional practice. Whether or not a journal is peer-reviewed should be indicated on its web site or in the front or back matter of its print edition. This information is also available by way of *Ulrichsweb*, and to a lesser degree in *Cabell's Directory of Publishing Opportunities in Educational Technology and Library Science* and in the *LIS Publications Wiki*. Authors are also encouraged to identify relevant scholarly publications for their work by conducting subject heading-based searches in LIS databases (see Journal Databases section) and by limiting their results to peer-reviewed journal articles.

4.2 *Types of Articles*

Scholarly Articles

Scholarly LIS journals characteristically include one or more of several types of articles. Authors must consider what type of article they are writing, and whether or not that work is appropriate for the journals they are considering.

Most journals will include information about the types of articles they prefer to publish on their web sites or in the front or back matter of their print editions. Authors are also encouraged to review several issues of the journals they are considering; each publication has its own unique style for the types of articles that they prefer. Listed below are descriptions of the common types of articles published in scholarly LIS journals.

Bibliographies. The intended audience of LIS professionals will likely know that bibliographies are lists of works compiled by a common organizing principle, such as authorship, subject, chronology, or place of publication. When presented as journal articles, these works are almost always annotated. Bibliographies, however, are not commonly published in scholarly LIS journals. There are exceptions: The journal, *Reference Services Review*, publishes annual annotated bibliographies of recently published works on the combined topic of library instruction and information literacy. Still, it is important to note that this type of article rarely undergoes a formal review process, even when published in a peer-reviewed journal. Prospective authors who have enough material to compile a bibliography are encouraged to develop their work into a more impactful review article instead (see Reviews section).

Case Studies. Commonly known as "how we did it well" pieces, case studies articles are those that demonstrate best practices in librarianship. Since LIS is largely an applied discipline, its professional literature includes a relatively high percentage of this type of work. Case studies include presentations and discussions of new, innovative, and effective practices that have taken place in a specific type of library, in a functional area of that type of library, and involving specialists within that functional area. There is an ongoing demand for these types of works, particularly if they involve activities that can be replicated to improve professional practice in similar library settings elsewhere. Consequently, there are numerous LIS journals devoted to each type of library, to each functional area within different types of libraries, and to each professional specialty within each functional area; the publishers of these journals are always looking for effective and well-written case studies.

It is important to note that case study articles are sometimes published in non-refereed LIS periodicals as well. Scholarly case articles are distinguished by features that should be familiar to LIS professionals. Specifically, scholarly cases are written in a formal, prescribed format that generally includes the following elements: abstract, introduction, description of the case, assessment of the case, results or implications, discussion, conclusions, and references to other relevant works. Based on the nature of the subject matter, case articles may also include a literature review or method section, too. When appropriate to do so, authors are highly encouraged to include a literature review, thereby establishing the usefulness of their case and demonstrating its noteworthiness within the greater body of LIS literature.

Perspectives Pieces. As readers will infer from the name, perspectives pieces are articles in which authors discuss their assertions, beliefs, experiences, opinions, philosophies, reflections, and theories relative to the scope and subject matter of a particular journal. These works differ from editorials in two significant ways: Whereas editorials are characteristically shorter works that are most often written by journal editors or regular columnists, perspectives pieces are lengthier, more thoughtful explorations that are most often written by authors who are unaffiliated with the journals in which their works appear. Perspectives pieces can be invited works—particularly in the instance of special or theme issues—or they can be uninvited works. Sometimes journal editors will deem uninvited manuscript submissions to be more appropriate as perspectives pieces than as feature articles. In such instances, an editor will typically ask for the author's permission to publish the work as a perspectives piece instead of a featured work. The key distinction is that perspectives pieces rarely undergo a formal review process, even when they are published in peer-reviewed journals.

Research Articles. Research articles are reports on the outcomes of studies that were conducted and the supporting data that was collected. These works are strict presentations of facts—as opposed to opinions or summaries of existing literature—and they are written by and for other practitioners and researchers for the purpose of making specific findings known to a targeted LIS community at large. Research articles are the most formally presented types of works; they follow a highly formalized and prescribed structure, style, and tone. Depending on the nature of the studies conducted, research papers will typically include the following elements: abstract, introduction, literature review, methods, results, discussion, conclusions, and references. Library and information science journals publish two types of research articles:

> **Quantitative Research Articles.** Quantitative research papers are reports on studies that were conducted by way of statistical, mathematical, or computational methods. The most common of these research methods in LIS is statistical. The objective of this type of work is to answer questions of *what*, *where*, and *when*, and then to create models, theories, and hypotheses related to the subject matter of the author's area of research. Typically, the LIS researcher asks a specific question or investigates a specific phenomenon, and then collects statistical data to answer the question or to explain the phenomenon. The challenge of this type of research is to collect data that yields unbiased results, which can then be applied to create improved models of professional practice.

> **Qualitative Research Articles.** Qualitative research papers are reports on studies that were conducted by way of observing human behavior. The objective of this type of work is to answer questions of *why* and *how* that are related to human behavior, and to understand the reasons or motivations for it. For LIS researchers, the most common qualitative studies are related to library user behavior. The nature of conducting qualitative research typically necessitates the use of smaller research samples than those used in quantitative studies. As such, the challenge of this type of research is to collect data on a comparatively smaller scale than quantitative work, and to apply the resulting conclusions to answer questions and to support hypotheses in a broader professional context.

> **Response Articles.** As the name suggests, these types of articles are responses to previously published works, usually from the same journal. These papers are typically shorter and easier to write than other types of articles, because

they are focused solely on one previously published work instead of the entire body of disciplinary literature. Response articles are not common in LIS literature, but logic holds that journal editors would welcome those that are thoughtful and well-written. These types of articles can generate lively and healthy debate within the discipline, thus resulting in increased attention paid to the journals they are published in. Prospective authors considering this type of paper are forewarned to be professional and respectful, and not to trounce on previously published works. The community of LIS scholars is relatively small and closely-knit; one's reputation can be easily tarnished by authoring an abrasive response article. It is also worth noting that these types of articles rarely undergo a formal review process, even when published in peer-reviewed journals.

Review Articles. These articles present reviews of specific topics from the body of a disciplinary literature. Authors sometimes confuse the format and purpose of review papers with those of bibliographies. Whereas the latter is simply an annotated list of works on a given topic, review papers include critical analyses of that topic as presented in the literature. These types of works should discuss the strengths of topical coverage, but they should also highlight the shortcomings, the gaps, and the contradictions. They should also include thoughtful, informed suggestions for future directions and research. Although review articles are not as common as case studies or research papers in the overall body of LIS literature, they are highly valued works. Importantly, these articles almost always undergo a formal review process.

Theoretical Articles. Theoretical articles present reviews, criticisms, and proposed changes to a specific theory from a discipline, or from an area of study or practice. These works typically provide the history and development of a given theory, a rationale for modification, and then a specific theoretical proposition. Proposed changes can involve debunking, revising, or advancing a given theory. Such articles are less commonly featured in LIS journals than case studies and research papers, but they can be considered highly valuable additions to the overall body of literature. More often than not they undergo a formal review process, but journal editors will sometimes prefer to publish these works as unreviewed perspectives pieces.

4.3 *Journal Rankings*

Ranking Systems

There are increasingly numerous journal ranking systems in use today. For decades the standard ranking for many academics and researchers was impact factor, but in recent years Eigenfactor score and H-index have emerged as competing alternatives. Each of these rankings has its own strengths and weakness, and supporters and detractors. There are numerous methods for determining journal rankings, and the various definitions and formulas involved can be complicated and confusing. These methods are commonly referred to as bibliometrics, citation metrics, or scientometrics— terms that refer to the quantitative measurement and analysis of a body of literature in an effort to determine overall impact. This is a burgeoning area of practice and research, not just in LIS, but within most academic disciplines. The tools that are used to determine journal rankings are both sophisticated and imperfect, and the implications depend primarily on the needs, desires, and expectations of authors. The purpose of the sections to follow is to explain in a simple way the terms, tools, and measures that are most commonly used for journal rankings, with a particular emphasis on the needs of LIS professionals.

Impact Factor. Impact factor is a journal ranking system devised by Eugene Garfield, the founder of the Institute for Scientific Information, which is now a part of Thomson Reuters. This ranking is calculated yearly for journals that are indexed in the *Journal Citation Reports* (JCR) database, which is powered by the *Web of Science*. A journal's impact factor refers to a given year of publication, and to the average number of citations received per article in that journal during the two preceding years. Let us use the journal, *Information Systems Research*, and the publication year 2010 as an example. Its 2010 impact factor of 3.358 means that articles published in the journal during 2008 and 2009 were cited, on average, 3.358 times in other journals that are indexed in JCR.[7] The JCR database also provides a five-year impact factor that works the same way, but uses the previous five years of publication instead. Simply put, journals that receive higher citation rates among other journals indexed in JCR are ranked higher than those that do not.

For some disciplines—especially those in the sciences—impact factor is a standard instrument for ranking journals. The same is true for many institutions, and even for individual academic departments. However, the use of or reliance on impact factor also generates numerous criticisms. The primary criticisms involve the limited body of literature used for citation analysis, limited coverage of journals in the social sciences and the humanities, questions of validity (Rossner, Van Epps, & Hill, 2007), and the ability of authors, editors, and publishers to manipulate the system (Monastersky, 2005; Grant, 2010). All of these criticisms, combined with the calculi cited below and the advent of new bibliographic searching tools, lead some scholars to assert that impact factor may no longer be a sufficient indicator for determining the relative impact and value of journals (Meho & Yang, 2007).

The 2010 edition of JCR includes citation analyses for 10,196 journals (Thomson Reuters, 2011); based on a search of the *Ulrichsweb* serials directory, this equates to roughly 20 percent of currently active, scholarly journals.[8] Of particular note to LIS professionals, the 2010 edition of JCR indexes just 77 library and information science journals, and there is only a modest overlap of included titles with those that are deemed by library directors and library school deans to be the most prestigious in the discipline (see Journal Prestige section).

As noted, deciding which journal is currently most fitting for one's work is critical. Impact factor can be an important consideration for some authors, perhaps for the purpose of achieving promotion or tenure. However, it is important to recognize that by virtue of its own formula for calculation, impact factor can be considered dated information. A journal's 2009 impact factor, for example, cannot be calculated until all of that year's publications have been processed; that information is appears in the 2010 edition of JCR. Journals newly selected for indexing in JCR, starting with a volume other than the first, will not receive an impact factor for three years. Furthermore, new journals, indexed from their first volume, will not receive an impact factor for two years; in this instance, citations to the year prior to the first volume and to the number of articles published in the year prior to the first volume are given zero values.

Eigenfactor Score. Eigenfactor is a journal ranking system developed by Jevin West, Carl Bergstrom, Ben Althouse, Martin Rosvall, and Ted Bergstrom.

This system ranks the importance of journals through citation analysis, but in a similar manner to the way that *Google* ranks web pages. Whereas the *Google* algorithm uses the network of hyperlinks on the free web, Eigenfactor uses the network of citations in journals that are indexed in JCR. The purpose is to identify the influence of journals within the network of scholarly literature. An *Eigenfactor* score represents the number of times articles from a journal published in the past five years have been cited in a JCR year. Let us use the journal, *Journal of the American Informatics Association*, and the publication year 2010 as an example. Its 2010 Eigenfactor score of 0.01257 means that articles published in the journal from 2005-2009 were cited, on average, 0.01257 times during 2010 in other journals that are indexed in JCR.[9]

Eigenfactor score is considered by some scholars to be more robust than impact factor because, with the former, journals are ranked by more than just the number of citations received; citations from highly ranked journals are given greater weight than those from poorly ranked journals. The Eigenfactor formula also removes references from one article in a journal to another article in the same journal, thus eliminating the problem of self-citations. The developers of this system assert that a single citation from a highly ranked journal may be more valuable than multiple citations from peripheral publications. As described by Bergstrom (2007), Eigenfactor measures "the importance of a citation by the influence of the citing journal *divided by the total number of citations appearing in that journal*" (p. 314). The ultimate purpose of Eigenfactor is to provide a measurement of likelihood that a given journal will be used by average researchers in the same field. Journal rankings are freely available at the Eigenfactor web site (http://www.eigenfactor.org/); they are also provided alongside impact factor in the JCR database.

In terms of criticism, Davis (2008) argued that Eigenfactor score is insufficiently different from impact factor to warrant its status as a new and useful journal ranking system. West, Bergstrom, and Bergstrom (2010) countered that argument with an analysis of their own that suggests otherwise. Regardless, LIS authors who are comparing and contrasting Eigenfactor score and impact factor should remember the key shortcomings of both rankings: namely, the limited body of literature used for citation analysis, the actual coverage of LIS journals, and the currency of data used for calculations.

H-Index. Alternatively known as Hirsch index or Hirsch number, H-index was proposed by physicist, Jorge E. Hirsch. It is a multipurpose formula commonly used to measure the impact and productivity of individual scholars, academic departments, schools, universities, research institutions, and even countries. Apropos of the present text, H-index was expanded, allowing for it to also be used as a measure of the scholarly impact of journals. As Hirsch (2005) described, the index is calculated as, "the number of papers with citation number $\geq h$" (p. 16569). In lay terminology, an author's H-index is the intersection of where the number of his or her published papers meets the number of citations to those papers. Banks and Dellavalle (2008) provided a useful illustration of how this is calculated and applied:

> An author with an h index of 30 has published 30 papers that received at least 30 citations in subsequent work. If one scholar has published 100 papers and another has published 35, but both have 30 papers that received 30 citations, each would have an h index of 30. (p. 169)

Noting the inconsistencies of using impact factor for ranking journals in different disciplines, Barendse (2007) proposed building on H-index with a logarithm called strike rate index (SRI). This allowed for journals in different disciplines to be compared objectively, and it transformed H-index from a measurement of individual scholars, departments, and institutions into an important instrument for evaluating journals.

A journal's H-index will vary, sometimes significantly, depending on the body of literature used to collect and analyze citations. The most commonly used sources are *Web of Science, Scopus* and *Google Scholar. Web of Science's* coverage of scholarly literature, and LIS in particular, is highly selective. As a result, journal H-indices are likely to be lower than those provided by *Scopus* and *Google Scholar.* Coverage of the literature provided by *Scopus* is not comprehensive, but it is more substantial than that provided by *Web of Science.* This is the body of literature used to inform *SCImago Journal &*

Country Rank (SJR), which is a free web journal ranking system available at http://www.scimagojr.com/. Currently, SJR provides H-indices for 134 LIS journals.[10] *Google Scholar* currently provides the broadest coverage of scholarly literature from which to glean bibliographic information and calculate a journal's H-index. This is the data source used to provide H-indices for individuals and journals in the *Harzing's Publish or Perish* program, which may be freely downloaded from http://www.harzing.com/pop.htm.

As with impact factor and Eigenfactor score, the use of H-index generates criticisms. Many of these criticisms are particular to the ranking of individual scholars, but some apply to the ranking of journals, too. H-index, for instance, does not account for the number of citations typically used in articles for different disciplines, nor does it account for excessive citations that may appear in review articles. If it is necessary for authors to use ranking systems to select journals in which to publish, they are encouraged to use more than one system, and then to compare and contrast the results from each; this should help to provide a more accurate and comprehensive outlook in terms of overall journal impact and quality.

Journal Prestige

As with impact factor, Eigenfactor score, and H-index, the prestige attributed to any journal should be considered in the context of the professional needs and desires of authors. For some LIS professionals the processes of earning appointments, promotions, and tenure are based partly on their record of publishing in highly ranked or prestigious journals. The publishing expectations for LIS authors and the attributed measures of journal prestige differ from institution to institution, particularly for library practitioners. Faculty library educators are more likely to have more uniform professional expectations, but those will also vary from school to school. Prospective authors may be required to publish in "leading" or "top-tier" journals, based on specific bibliometrics or ranking schemes, or they may simply need to publish in any peer-reviewed journals. Research by Best and Kneip (2010) showed that 52.8 percent of academic libraries require their librarians to publish in scholarly journals, 33.7 percent encourage the practice, and 13.5 have no such requirement (p. 104). The authors of this study also suggested that "librarians at academic institutions tend to publish more frequently in top-tier journals" (p. 97). This should prompt the following questions: What constitutes a top-tier journal? How do the 86.5 percent of institutions requiring or encouraging their librarians to publish measure or attribute prestige to journals? The answer to both of these questions is the same: It differs from institution to institution, and it is based largely on professional perceptions.

There is only modest overlap of LIS journals that are ranked highly by way of the systems described earlier in the text and those publications that are perceived to be the most prestigious by leaders within the profession of librarianship. Kohl and Davis (1985) conducted a cornerstone study, in which they surveyed LIS school deans and Association of Research Libraries (ARL) directors to collect their perceptions of the prestige of core library and information science journals. The authors found a general agreement among the deans and directors for ranking two-thirds of the journals presented, but there was considerable disagreement regarding the remaining titles. Additional findings showed more agreement among LIS deans than among ARL directors (p. 40).

The findings above can be explained to a certain degree by considering the different motivations and professional expectations of prospective authors from both groups. It is logical to assume that library school deans rate LIS education journals highly, and that ARL directors are likely to perceive professional practice titles as being more important. Furthermore, professional expectations, in terms of publishing, promotion, and tenure, are more uniform among LIS educators than among ARL librarians. Professional expectations for ARL librarians will vary considerably from institution to institution. More to the point, the intended audience of this text should weigh the fact that ARL institutions represent only a small fraction of academic libraries, and that their motivations for publishing in specific journals may not align with those of their ARL colleagues.

The Kohl and Davis study was replicated by Blake (1996), and then again by Nisonger and Davis (2005). Results of both studies showed some continuity with the original Kohl and Davis work; they confirmed a general hierarchy of prestige among LIS journals, and they showed significant perception gaps between the two survey populations. Nisonger and Davis offer the following two analyses for prospective authors who may be considering, comparing, and contrasting LIS journal ranking systems and perceptions of prestige:

> A weak to moderate correlation was found between deans' ratings and *Journal Citation Reports* citation scores, whereas the correlation between directors' perceptions and citation data were weak to nonexistent. (p. 341)

> Journal value is multifaceted, so that a low-ranking journal in this study may still be important for supporting teaching, professional practice, a specialty area, or some other purpose. (p. 375)

Another important conclusion to draw from the studies above is that perceptions of journals from both survey groups change over time. This reinforces previous assertions of ongoing changes in the profession—as reflected in the literature—and also of the importance that should be attributed to selecting journals that are currently most relevant and appropriate for an author's scholarly work.

As with the journal ranking systems described, these studies have shortcomings: most notably, the limited number of journal titles included. Only 31 titles were used in the original Kohl and Davis study; these were selected from an article in Shera's authoritative text, *Introduction to Library Science* (1976). Kohl and Davis's methodology also excluded "special-interest" journals, and those that were not published in the United States (p. 41). The subsequent 1996 and 2005 studies replicated this methodology, but made slight accommodations to expand the number of titles included, and also to account for discontinued journals.

Unlike the ranking systems described, these studies constitute a discipline-specific attempt to evaluate journal quality. However, it is safe to conclude that these studies do not constitute a comprehensive evaluation or ranking of LIS journals. It is also clear that the study conclusions may or may not be relevant to prospective authors. Authors are highly encouraged to give greater weight to their own motivations in terms of selecting the appropriate journal for their work. Selecting the right journal should be based on a variety of factors; ranking and prestige may or may not be a part that equation. Authors should have a complete understanding of their own institutions' written policies regarding professional expectations, especially concerning publication requirements. Of equal importance, authors should also consult with their unit heads, supervisors, and directors; the experience and expertise of these individuals should serve as critical guidance.

4.4 *Journal Publishers*

Types of Journal Publishers

Authors who are vetting journals as potential outlets for their work need to consider interrelated issues concerning publisher type, authority, and reputation. These can be straight-forward considerations that are based on author experiences, preferences, or professional expectations. However, they can also be complicated, and can strike at the heart of LIS professional philosophy and responsibility. Authors reviewing potential journals should begin the process by determining publisher type, and then consider the relative implications. Different publisher types are detailed below:

Commercial Publishers. Commercial publishers are first and foremost for-profit companies. They are unaffiliated with colleges, universities, or professional associations, and as such, they have no particular allegiance to those entities. Instead, they have disciplinary or subject area niches; that is their specialty in the scholarly journal marketplace. Larger commercial publishers are often multidisciplinary, but even then, they are typically more focused on niche audiences in the sciences, in the social sciences, or in the arts and humanities.

Many LIS professionals believe that commercial publishers leverage their position in the marketplace to wield monopolistic authority, and that they use that authority to exploit academic libraries through unwarranted journal price inflation. A complex, interwoven, and recalcitrant set of factors allow for this to occur. The key factor is copyright law, which protects publishers who require authors to cede ownership of their own work, prevents competition for acquiring scholarly works in the marketplace, and forces libraries to purchase materials from publishers who will exploit them. Historically, the problem of price inflation has been with scientific, technical, and medical (STM) journals (Schlimgen & Kronefeld, 2004). However, evidence shows that when libraries are forced by budgetary challenges to cancel high-priced STM subscriptions, commercial publishers compensate by simultaneously increasing the subscription prices for journals in other disciplines, including LIS (Hollister, 2001).

To be fair, commercial publishers of scholarly serials provide a necessary service, the production quality of their print and electronic journals is consistently first-rate, and they provide some of the most important and prestigious LIS titles. Additionally, as LIS professionals know, the historical relationship between scholars, publishers, and libraries was once beneficial to all parties. During the 1970s, however, some commercial publishers "discovered that library demands for journals were remarkably unresponsive to price increases and that publishers could greatly increase their revenues by sharply increasing their prices" (Bergstrom and McAfee, 2005). Thus began a precipitous disintegration of a once beneficial relationship. Today, academics commonly and openly refer to commercial publishers as enemies in the world of scholarly communication (Taylor, 2012).

Large publishing empires, like Elsevier, Wiley & Sons, and Wolters Kluwer are the most blatant offenders in terms of gouging libraries, but the good news for LIS authors is that the collective foci of these publishers are mainly in the STM disciplines. Only a small percentage of LIS journals come from these large corporations. As a general rule, the most prominent commercial publishers of scholarly LIS journals do not press their advantage to the extent described; these include Emerald, Routledge, and Taylor & Francis. Additionally, there are many, comparatively small commercial presses, like Allerton, McFarland & Company, and Scarecrow, that publish small numbers of LIS serials. Authors who are considering journals from commercial publishers are encouraged to investigate their relative histories of price inflation, and to compare those titles and histories with similar journals from other types of publishers.

University Publishers. Like commercial publishers, university presses are for-profit companies, but as their names suggest, they are university-affiliated, and they are also in the business of academia. As such, their exploitation of the academic library marketplace tends to be far less egregious. In terms of the scholarly journal marketplace, university presses generally do not have disciplinary or subject area niches. Those that publish LIS journals typically offer just one or two titles based on the scholarly strengths at their respective institutions. As a general rule, university presses are multidisciplinary, but they tend to more heavily focused on the social sciences and the arts and humanities.

As a result of differing business models, university presses have less money than commercial publishers to devote to production quality. Still, their print and electronic products are highly professional, and university presses provide many of the LIS journals that are consistently ranked highest in terms of impact and prestige. Among the most prominent of these publishers are Johns Hopkins University, Oxford University, and University of Chicago; but there are many others.

Professional Association Publishers. Professional association publishers operate as part of a larger nonprofit organization. They publish journals devoted to advancing the professions or areas of research and study that the larger organization represents; that is their niche. As examples, the Association for Library and Information Science Education publishes *Journal of Education for Library and Information Science*, the Association of College and Research Libraries publishes *College & Research Libraries*, the Medical Library Association publishes *Journal of the Medical Library Association*, and so on. The target audience for these journals is predominantly the membership of the larger professional organization; members usually receive copies as a benefit of their affiliation.

By virtue of their nonprofit status, professional association publishers tend to be less expensive and less exploitative than other types of presses, and for reasons that should resonate with the intended reader of this text, that is particularly the case for LIS journals. Although their trade magazines are usually attractive, colorful, and fancy, professional association presses generally have less money than other types of publishers to devote to production quality of their scholarly journals. Still, their print and electronic products are highly professional, and they provide many of the LIS titles that are consistently ranked highest in the discipline in terms of impact and prestige.

Independent Publishers. As a result of fundamental, rapid, and ongoing changes in the world of scholarly communication, new and independent models of journal publishing have emerged. Like other types of publishers, independents operate to advance particular areas of professional practice, research and study, but they do so either partly of completely outside the traditional system of journal publishing. Independent publishers are motivated by a combination of passion for the subject matter in their journals, the potential they recognize in new and innovative methods for the dissemination of scholarly communication, and disenchantment with elements of the traditional system of journal publishing. These motivations are often shared by authors who elect to publish their works in independent journals.

The variables in place that allow for independents to publish journals on their own terms include advancements in communication and information technologies, new and flexible models for copyright licensing (see Copyright section), and evolving attitudes toward scholarly communication. As compared to academics from other disciplines, and by virtue of their core professional skills and values, LIS professionals are ahead of the curve in terms of embracing the new models of scholarly communication that are developed by independent publishers.

By definition, independent journal publishers are unaffiliated with any commercial enterprises, educational institutions, or professional associations. Often these presses are created and managed by just one or two practitioners or researchers in a given field. Independents can be for-profit or nonprofit, but they are primarily the latter of the two, and more often than not their products are open access journals (see Open Access Journals section). Independents use elements of the traditional journal publishing system that they believe in, and discard or replace elements that they do not. The production quality of these publications varies considerably, which is largely the result of available staffing, time, and money.

LIS Journal Publishers. There is a general assumption of scholarly communication that journals from large, well-known commercial and university publishers are considered to be more stable, and by extension, more authoritative and prestigious. There is also a general assumption that journals from university publishers tend to be more prestigious than those from other types of publishers. However, these assumptions do not necessarily hold for LIS journals. To begin, larger commercial and university presses do not have a dominant presence in library literature. Relatively small commercial and university publishers provide a higher number and wider range of the specialized journals that LIS professionals and researchers require. Also, when compared to the literature other disciplines, LIS has a greater number of highly ranked scholarly journals from professional association publishers. As Nisonger and Davis (2005) show, the top twenty LIS journals, in terms of perceived prestige by LIS education deans and ARL library directors, include a greater number of titles from professional association publishers. This number is followed closely by commercial, and then university presses.

Finally, as the world of scholarly communication continues to evolve, authors should consider how their works will be found and used in the future. The best way to anticipate this is to identify current trends, and then to use that information to project forward. Advances in communication and information technologies continue to revolutionize the world of scholarly communication. Academics and researchers are increasingly dependent on easy, fast, and seamless access to information by way of their preferred electronic devices and desktops. For this reason, the traditional model of scholarly publishing, which prevents seamless access to information, is likely to continue undergoing profound changes. The prominence of the free web will continue to grow among scholars, as will the influence of journals that are freely available there (i.e., open access journals). Although other types of publishers will continue their ineluctable, but reticent march toward open access, independent publishers are already thriving there, and their influence is also likely to grow in the scholarly community.

Publication Medium and Model

Medium. An electronic platform for one's published work is a mandatory prerequisite for authors who are vetting journals. Most publishers continue to publish print and electronic editions of their journals, and that is perfectly fine. Indeed, many academics prefer to read their literature in print. However, more and more journals are electronic only, and more and more are born that way. No serious academic can refute the fact that the world of scholarly communication has gone largely electronic. This statement holds true for the discipline of library and information science, too; any LIS journals worthy of consideration for one's work are either electronic, or have electronic editions. Naturally, this leads to issues of indexing and dissemination, which are discussed later in this chapter.

Model. The matter of publication model is increasingly an important consideration for today's scholars. Specifically, the issue is whether or not one should submit their work to subscription-based or to open access publications. For some authors the consideration is driven principally by professional expectations and what is stipulated by their institutions for achieving appointment, promotion, and tenure; this ties in with matters of journal rankings and perceived prestige (see Journal Rankings section earlier in this chapter). For others, the primary concern is the dissemination of their work, and the ease of access to it for their peers. Of course, these two considerations are not mutually exclusive.

For a growing constituency of authors the matter of publication model is also an important philosophical consideration. This is particularly true for LIS professionals, who know very well the consequences to their institutions of journal price inflation, and whose collective professional philosophy of access to information runs counter to the barriers that often come by way of subscription-based journals. The particular implications of publishing in subscription or open access journals are discussed in the following sections.

Subscription Journals

A detailed and lengthy description of subscription-based scholarly journals is unnecessary for the intended audience of LIS professionals, who are already experts in the area by virtue of their daily responsibilities. This model of scholarly publishing is well established (see History of Scholarly Papers section), and it is understandable that prospective authors will select subscription-based journals for numerous personal and professional reasons, but among those reasons are comfort, familiarity, and predisposition. That is to say, authors are accustomed to an established system of scholarly communication that affords them a set of necessary benefits in terms of publication and dissemination, and because of this, they may naturally be inclined to continue publishing in the same manner.

The advantages of publishing in subscription-based journals are manifold. Publishers that operate on this model offer the necessary, market-driven variety of reputable and specialized journals for scholars in all areas of study; they create the actual end products of authors' scholarly work; and they have well-established methods and systems of indexing and dissemination. By virtue of these strengths, the traditions of publishing scholarly papers, and the protections provided by copyright law, the subscription-based journal model will unquestionably continue for the foreseeable future.

The disadvantages of publishing in the subscription-based journals are also manifold. Scholarly literature that comes by way of this publication model continues to be characterized by accessibility barriers, outdated modes of visibility, inconveniences associated with traditional methods of information retrieval, and predatory price inflation. Significant and ongoing changes in the world of scholarly communication should prompt authors to reconsider the overall purpose of publishing their work, and to select the model of publication that it best suited to satisfy their professional goals, objectives, and philosophies.

Open Access Journals

Open access journals are defined simply as scholarly serials that are freely available to anyone with access to the Internet. Prospective authors should consider many aspects and implications of publishing in open access journals, including visibility, measures of impact and prestige, differing operational models, future directions for scholarly communication, and even professional values and philosophy. To begin, open access journals are, in the current research environment, far more visible to scholars than those in print; they exist without the accessibility barriers that come with costly, subscription-based source materials; and they have none of the familiar inconveniences associated with the traditional model of information retrieval. The rapidly expanding relationship between researchers and the free web is cyclical; the increasing use of the free web for research means that more and more scholarly information will be made freely available, and as a result, scholars will rely more and more on those materials that they can easily find and retrieve online.

A multitude of bibliometric studies illustrate the citation advantage of publishing in open access journals (Open Citation Project, 2012). Eysenbach (2006) conducted a pivotal study in this area, comparing the impact of open access and non-open access articles appearing in the same journal. His findings showed that open access articles are more immediately found and cited by researchers, even with those appearing in journals that are widely available in academic libraries. More recently, and more germane to the intended audience, Xia (2012) used H-index as a metric to rank LIS journals, and to "assess current OA [open access] development in support of scholarly communication" (p. 134). Results of this study showed the following:

> Several OA journals have been rated as high as the best traditional non-OA journals. Considering the relative short history of the open access movement, the achievements of these OA journals are not exaggerated. This encouraging news is good for the ongoing promotion of the new means of digital scholarly communication among researchers. (p. 143)

There are differing operational models for managing and maintaining open access journals, which may or may not have an impact on potential contributors. Some publications are funded by academic institutions, professional associations, or governmental agencies (see Publisher

Authority section). Others require author fees, or article processing charges. The latter of these economic models assumes that contributors have sufficient grant money or institutional backing to cover those costs. This is unlikely to affect LIS researchers; more often than not this scenario involves researchers in scientific, technical, and medical (STM) disciplines. There is also a small but growing percentage of open access journals that operate successfully on revenues generated from miscellaneous other sources, like grants, print-on-demand services, professional donations, and royalties from indexing contracts with subscription database vendors.

In the process of selecting the right journal, authors should reflect on how their scholarly works will potentially be found and used in the future. They should consider the rapid, fundamental, ongoing, and inevitable changes in the methods of conducting research. Contemporary researchers rely on what the free web has to offer, and that reliance will continue to grow. Furthermore, the very idea of publishing in open access journals should resonate with LIS professionals; it helps to relieve libraries of the continuing burden of exploitative scholarly serial price inflation; it helps to build the credibility, and thus, the prestige of open access publications; and it encourages other researchers to similarly contribute with their own works. Open access is at the heart of LIS professional philosophy, which supports, above all else, seamless access to information for all.

Open access journals represent a new paradigm for the process of scholarly communication; it is understandable that some authors, institutions, and even academic disciplines are reluctant to embrace it. Regardless, the growth of the open access continues apace and unabated. The *Directory of Open Access Journals* (DOAJ: available at http://www.doaj.org/) was formed in 2003 to boost the visibility of open access scholarly journals, thus promoting their increased usage and overall impact. Currently, DOAJ includes over 8,500 journals, and 137 LIS titles.[11] Influential organizations like the *Scholarly Publishing and Academic Resources Coalition* (SPARC: available at http://www.arl.org/sparc/) continue in their efforts to correct imbalances in the scholarly journal system, to advocate for new models of scholarly communication, and to reduce the financial pressures on libraries exerted by the commercial publishers of scholarly periodical literature.

Prestigious institutions like Harvard University (2008) and professional organizations like the Association of American Universities (2009) are leading efforts to bring scholarship to the free web. The momentum of open access has even resulted in significant actions taken by federal lawmakers, as with the National Institutes of Health Public Access Policy in the Consolidated Appropriations Act (2008), and the recently reintroduced Federal Research Public Access Act (S. 2096, 2012), which was endorsed by 52 Nobel Laureates (Abrikosov et al., 2012).

Publication History

The checklist for deciding whether or not a journal is suitable for one's scholarly work should include a review of its publication history. Authors are encouraged to review how long a journal has been in existence, how consistently issues are published, and whether or not there is a history of changes, delays, or interruptions in its publication schedule. Authors are also recommended to investigate whether or not a journal in question has undergone any significant changes in direction, dissemination, editorship, publisher, publishing model, scope, or target audience. Although none on these variables are absolute determinants, they are, to some extent, traditional measures of stability.

Notwithstanding the assumed good standing of journals with longer or unchanged publishing histories, authors should not dismiss the great prospects and vital importance of newer journals, or those that have recently undergone significant changes. As with any discipline, practice, or area of study, change is a constant, it is essential, and it should be reflected in the relative professional literature. Authors are also encouraged to investigate the credentials, diversity, and experience of a journal's editor, its editorial board, and its recently published authors. It is an imperative, particularly for newer journals, to demonstrate their authority by way of experienced and scholarly associations; these criteria help to build a journal reputations, and thus, to imbue author confidence, and to attract greater numbers of higher caliber manuscript submissions.

Production Quality

In some respects, the appearance, copyediting, and physical or electronic presentation of a journal are reliable determinants in terms of overall quality, and in other respects they are not. That is to say, if a journal consistently exhibits production flaws, such as substandard writing, typos, incorrect or missing references, mismatched fonts, uneven or imbalanced text, poor quality figures and illustrations, or other signs of neglect, it is very likely not a well-respected publication. The same holds for the physical or electronic presentation of a journal. A print edition presented on cheap, thin paper, or an electronic edition with poor design or navigation, is also likely to lack reputability. These publications are often developed and managed by bright, dedicated, and well-meaning practitioners or researchers, but these professionals characteristically lack the financing and necessary staffing and time that is required for producing authoritative scholarly journals.

It is important to note, however, that professional copyediting, expensive paper stock, and fancy design are not absolute indicators of overall journal quality. Even the largest and wealthiest commercial publishers include well-produced journals that are not particularly well-regarded in their respective catalogs, and even the most prestigious and elegantly produced journals will sometimes include errors that slip through the cracks during the copyediting process. As a general rule, commercial publishers have more money, staff, and time to devote to production quality than university, professional association, and independent publishers. Although production is critically important, it is just one variable in the overall equation of vetting journal quality.

4.5 *Additional Journal Vetting*

Target Audience

In a sense, the process of selecting journals based on target audience is very much the same as selecting journals based on subject area and scope. Authors can begin their search by using the same sources described earlier in this chapter: *Ulrichsweb, WorldCat,* journal databases, *Cabell's Directory of Publishing Opportunities in Educational Technology and Library Science,* the *LIS Publications Wiki,* and the free web. Once a manageable number of prospective journals is identified, further vetting can commence. Clear and unambiguous statements of each journal's intended readership should be easily found on each its web site, or in the front or back matter of its print edition.

Authors are encouraged, however, to think differently in terms of intended audience; they should be focused more on the ultimate purpose of their work and less on the faceless readership of a seemingly appropriate journal. True scholarship is about more than simply publishing a paper to bolster one's dossier; it is about genuinely contributing to a body of knowledge, and to truly advancing one's discipline or practice. Authors should consider who will benefit the most from reading their work, and what publication will provide the most impact. If, for instance, an instruction librarian has written a paper about successfully integrating the teaching of information literacy skills into a college level history curriculum, then he or she should look beyond those LIS journals that simply publish articles on a wide spectrum of public services in academic libraries. In this case, the author should seek a journal that is focused specifically on teaching information literacy skills in higher education; that might include an LIS title, like *Communications in Information Literacy*, or a pedagogical journal from the history literature, like the *History Teacher*. Whereas the former title would reach a greater audience of fellow instruction librarians, the latter would be read by college history teachers, who might then be more inclined to forge collaborations with librarians at their own institutions. These are important considerations.

Writing Style

All scholarly journals require prospective authors to abide by a standard style of writing, formatting manuscripts, and citing sources. Chicago Style, as set forth in the *Chicago Manual of Style*, is most commonly used in LIS literature. American Psychological Association (APA) Style, as set forth in the *Publication Manual of the American Psychological Association*, is increasingly popular in the discipline, particularly with electronic-only journals. Some LIS journals require the use of formats that are developed specifically by their editors or their publishers, and combine them with different citation styles. For example, *Reference Services Review* requires prospective authors to format their papers in a specific style developed by Emerald for its journals, and to use Harvard Style for citing sources. As a general rule, however, the Chicago and APA Styles are the standards of the discipline. Stylistic requirements will be expressly stated on a journal's web site, or in the front or back matter of its print edition.

Most scholarly journals also exhibit characteristic or unique writing style subtleties that distinguish them from other publications in the discipline. Whereas some journals allow for flexibility in author tone, narration, title and heading conventions, formatting mechanics, and overall paper organization, others can be highly regimented. Authors are encouraged to review several issues of the journals they are considering in order to identify these preferred patterns of address, format, organization, and tone, and to consider whether or not they align with characteristics of their own writing.

Indexing and Dissemination

Although a variety of factors are involved in selecting a journal, prospective authors should remember that the ultimate purpose of publishing is to contribute to the LIS body of knowledge, and in so doing, to advance the discourse, theory, and practice of librarianship. This is the discipline-specific process of scholarly communication, and effective indexing and dissemination of one's work are crucial components. That is to say, publishing one's work is intellectually pointless if other practitioners and researchers do not have access to it.

The emergence of free web bibliographic searching tools like *Google Scholar* and *Microsoft Academic Search* have significantly changed the way research is conducted. However, publishers continue in their traditional role as essential partners in the process of scholarly communication. It is true that the controlling and exploitative practices of some journal publishers, particularly commercial ones, generate understandable measures of distrust and even contempt among librarians (see Publisher Authority section). Still, publishers provide an important and reliable infrastructure for indexing and dissemination.

The criteria for selecting a journal should include an examination of how accessible its contents are to other practitioners and researchers. Electronic accessibility is paramount. The intended audience of this text is encouraged to investigate whether or not the journals they are considering are indexed in the preeminent LIS subscription databases: *Library Literature & Information Science Full Text, Library, Information Science & Technology Abstracts with Full Text (LISTA), Library & Information Science Source,* and *Library and Information Science Abstracts (LISA).* If so, is the full-text of those journals available? What dates are covered, and is there an embargo period for recent volumes? Authors are also encouraged to investigate coverage provided by discipline-specific databases, by multidisciplinary databases, and also by the free web. The most authoritative source for providing this kind of information is *Ulrichsweb*. However, most publishers now have web sites that provide necessary, and often more current indexing and dissemination information. Authors can also use *WorldCat* to learn which and how many other institutions subscribe to journals they are considering.

Acceptance Rate

Far too much significance is given to the presumed relationship between manuscript acceptance rates and overall journal quality, and then by extension, to journal impact and prestige. Authors commonly equate low manuscript acceptance rates with high journal quality. Shelley and Schuh (2001) conducted a study that debunks this myth by showing that the quality of writing and readability is consistent from journals that are more selective to those that are less so (p. 17). The simple fact of the matter is that more LIS journals are being published today than ever before, and that many of them fail to attract and receive sufficient numbers of high-quality manuscript submissions. As Belcher (2009) asserts, "Although the increasing number of journals has been paired with an increasing number of productive faculty, the great secret of journal publishing is how often journals go begging for articles" (p. 101). There is even evidence to support the theory that journals are inaccurately reporting high manuscript rejection rates, particularly in the humanities and social sciences (Belcher, 2009, p. 101).

Authors are encouraged to focus more on selecting journals that are a good fit for their work, and less so on acceptance or rejection rates. Manuscripts are rejected for numerous reasons, but one of the most common of these is the proverbial poor fit. In any event, authors can investigate acceptance or rejection rates many ways. Some publications include that information on their web sites, or in the front or back matter of their print editions. The *Cabell's Directory of Publishing Opportunities in Educational Technology and Library Science* database includes acceptance rates for most of its profiled titles, but it does not provide comprehensive coverage of all LIS journals. Authors can also ask journal editors about acceptance rates in their query messages (see Querying Journal Editors section).

Submission Processes

Journals typically have strict rules for submitting manuscripts. Most LIS journals require electronic submission by way of uploading to their web site, or by sending as attachments through email. Some journals still stubbornly require multiple print copies to be sent through the mail, and a small number actually require both print and electronic submissions. Each publication will have specific rules for blinding manuscripts in advance of submission; these rules must be scrupulously followed. Most LIS journals accept unsolicited manuscripts, but authors are encouraged to query editors in advance (see Querying Journal Editors section). Doing this will help authors to further vet the journals they are considering, and it will help editors to anticipate manuscript submissions and to plan accordingly. Rules for submitting should be easily found on a journal's web site, or in the front or back matter of its print edition. For additional guidelines on the submission process, refer to the Manuscript Submission section.

Review Processes

Finding detailed information regarding the review processes for individual LIS journals is not always an easy task. Most scholarly journals have a double-blind review process in place for manuscripts submissions; that is, reviewers do not have access to personally or institutionally identifiable information about authors, and vice versa. Generally, editors will also see to it that reviewers are not privy to one another on given manuscript assignments. Editors will typically assign two or three reviewers for each manuscript submission. Assignments are based on reviewer profiles, interests, and expertise, and sometimes they are simply based on reviewer queues or availability. A handful of LIS journals have senior and junior level reviewers, and operate on a model that includes both in the review process for all submissions. This model is applied first and foremost as a measure of quality control. However, it is also used to assist in editorial decision making; when manuscript reviews are mixed, editors will give greater consideration to comments and suggestions provided by senior level reviewers.

The key for many authors is response time, or turnaround time for manuscript reviews. This process can be excruciatingly slow, and often it has little to do with the editor or the work flow operations of a journal. Simply put, reviewers can take a long time with their manuscript assignments. Much like the intended readers of this text, they are also busy LIS professionals. Still, it is the editor's job to keep reviewers on task and to encourage timely responses. As a general rule, most LIS journals have turnaround times of four to twelve weeks. Sometimes this information is disclosed on a journal's web site, or in the front or back matter of its print edition, but not always. Authors can also consult the *Cabell's Directory of Publishing Opportunities in Educational Technology and Library Science* database or the *LIS Publications Wiki* for estimated turnaround times. When all else fails, authors can query individual journal editors for this information.

Copyright

Traditional Copyright. Simply stated, copyright is the legal protection given to authors of original works. Copyright owners have the exclusive rights to control, distribute, perform, or reproduce those original works. The purpose of copyright law is not only to protect the rights of owners, but also to weigh those against the interests of users and the general public. However, the ownership of copyright relative to scholarly papers is a contentious issue for many authors; it can have profound implications and repercussions, and it can elicit strong opinions, particularly among LIS professionals. This is because copyright is often the mitigating factor that favors journal publishers when the interests of authors, publishers, and libraries compete or clash.

Under the traditional and most common model of publishing scholarly papers, authors are asked to cede the ownership rights of their own work as a condition of publication. Authors, who are often required to publish as a matter of their professional responsibilities, are forced to acquiesce, but this alone should not be too troubling. The primary concern for authors, beyond meeting requirements for appointment, promotion, and tenure, should be the professional packaging and the widest possible dissemination of their work. Under the traditional model of scholarly communication, dissemination occurs by way of publishers selling the professional packaging of authors' works to academic libraries through journal subscriptions. This is where the model breaks down.

Ideally, the cycle of scholarly communication should operate in a benign and mutually beneficial manner, with authors providing their work to publishers, with publishers providing the professional packaging of authors' work and selling it to libraries for a reasonable profit, and with libraries collecting the research collections that are necessary for authors to continue their work. The cycle of scholarly communication, however, is not ideal. Beginning in the 1980s some publishers began to leverage their ownership rights, under the protection of copyright law, in order to generate unreasonable profits through journal price inflation (see Commercial Publishers section). With little change and much controversy, this practice continues unabated today. The impact on libraries, and in turn, on scholars, is significant. Libraries—often operating on static or decreasing budgets—are driven by their own collection development policies and by the users they serve to acquire scholarly materials from publishers that exploit them. This is an unsustainable model; inevitably, libraries are forced to cancel journal subscriptions, and library collections are compromised. This, in turn, affects scholars who rely on libraries for their own research, and the cycle continues. Ultimately, greed is the culprit behind this dysfunctional model of publishing scholarly papers, but copyright law is the key variable that allows for it to continue.

Fortunately, LIS literature is not dominated by the types of publishers that most commonly abuse the traditional model of scholarly communication. Still, the aforementioned rule of ceding ownership rights remains a requirement for most publishers of all types, and that creates familiar and outdated barriers in terms of access and dissemination. For this reason, scholars are working within the framework of copyright law to develop methods and models of scholarly communication that are more advantageous in terms of access and dissemination, and more fitting of the Internet age.

Creative Commons (Available: http://creativecommons.org/). This non-profit organization was founded in 2001 in response to the realities of information use and flow in the Internet age. *Creative Commons* facilitates the freer dissemination and use of information by providing a variety of flexible, and easy to apply copyright licensing models. Licensing can stipulate, for instance, that authors retain ownership of their original work, but that others are free to copy, distribute, or make other non-commercial uses if it. Apropos of this chapter, journal publishers can use *Creative Commons* to develop their own licensing agreements for authors based on respective needs and expectations. Most LIS journals that adopt these licensing agreements are open access publications; they generally allow for authors to retain ownership rights to their work, but make other stipulations particular to the journal. As an example, the copyright notice for the open access journal, *Communications in Information Literacy* (CIL), reads as follows:

> Copyright for articles published in CIL is retained by the authors.
>
> Authors grant first publication rights to the journal and acknowledge that first publication includes publication in both print and electronic media, as well as the right to make the work available through an open access archive.
>
> Authors also extend to the Editors of *Communications in Information Literacy* the right to redistribute their articles via other scholarly resources and bibliographic databases at their discretion. This extension allows the authors' copyrighted content to be included in some databases that are distributed and maintained by for-profit companies. (Communications in Information Literacy, 2012)

Importantly, *Creative Commons* is not a replacement for copyright law; it is a flexible framework within it. Authors must recognize that copyright law exists to protect the rights of authors and the interests of the public at large, especially in areas of education, research, and access to information. In this spirit, as Hoorn (2005) asserted, "copyright serves the same interests as those inextricably linked with scholarly communication," and "This is why a practical first step to adjusting to an Open Access environment can be found within the existing framework of copyright law."

It is important to reiterate that LIS journal publishers generally operate on more benign business practices than those in other disciplines. The traditional model of publishing scholarly papers will continue, but authors are encouraged to consider how their work will be accessed and used in the future. If they have the professional latitude and institutional support to publish in journals that allow them to retain ownership of their work, they will likely increase the visibility and impact of that work among their peers in the profession. Publishing in this manner will also serve the greater good in terms of providing a model for scholars in other disciplines to emulate.

Institutional Repositories. Commonly referred to as an IR, the institutional repository is a digital collection of an institution's intellectual output. Most repositories are developed and maintained by colleges and universities for the purposes of collecting and preserving an institution's scholarly output in one location, providing open access to scholarly materials, and bolstering the visibility and impact of an institution's scholarship. Repositories also serve as visible locations for an institution's unpublished scholarly materials. By virtue of their professional expertise, librarians are often instrumental in the successful development and administration of repositories at their respective institutions.

The reason for including this information in the present text is to encourage authors to contribute their works to their respective institutional repositories. By doing so, authors are increasing the visibility and impact of their own work. Pushback from the scholarly community is forcing publishers to allow authors to include prepublication, and sometimes, modified post-publication copies of their works in repositories. This is considered to be fair use of copyrighted materials for the non-commercial purposes of advancing education, research, and scholarship. Authors who have already ceded ownership rights of their scholarly papers are required to obtain permission from journal publishers in order to contribute to their institutional repositories. However, it is increasingly common for authors to negotiate this type of agreement prior to signing the copyright transfer statements that publishers generally require.

Querying Journal Editors

Once an author has identified what appears to be the appropriate journal, he or she is highly encouraged to query the editor. Most LIS journals accept manuscripts that arrive without prior author contact; editors generally value them and treat them in the same professional manner as they do with manuscripts that arrive with prior author contact. However, the query serves several critically important purposes. To begin, it can either confirm or rebut one's findings in terms of matching his or her scholarly work to that journal. That matching begins with the specific subject matter of one's work, but it also extends to the type of manuscript, its conclusions, its methods, its timeliness, its estimated length, and any number of other elements that may be of particular concern to editors. Knowing ahead of time that a manuscript may or may not be the right fit for a journal saves time and energy for authors and editors alike.

The query is an opportunity for authors to ask questions that cannot be answered elsewhere during the journal vetting process. It is perfectly acceptable, for example, to ask editors how many manuscript submissions they receive per year, what their acceptance or rejections rates are, what the average turnaround time is for manuscript reviews, how long it takes from acceptance to publication, whether or not there is currently a backlog of manuscripts to be reviewed or articles to be published, and so on. The query is also an opportunity for authors to ask questions of clarification related to their manuscripts; these may be practical or technical questions related to paper formatting, submission processes, or other matters that are unclear in the author instructions area of a journal's web site or in the front or back matter of its print edition.

A golden rule of publishing is that authors should always make it as easy as possible for editors to do their work. In terms of the query, it should be professional, but above all things, it should be succinct. For ease-of-use and expediency, almost all LIS journal editors conduct their business through email. Authors are encouraged to contact them by way of the email address listed on the journal's web site or in its print edition; this may be different from an editor's institutional email address. The query should be formally addressed to the editor, and it should include the following elements:

- Brief note of any connections, such as previous meetings at conferences or mutual acquaintances
- Brief description of the purpose and unique nature of the manuscript
- Brief assertion of usefulness to the journal's target audience
- Indication of familiarity with and respect for the journal
- Reason for selecting the journal, and reason why the manuscript is an appropriate fit for it

- Manuscript title and abstract
- Estimated length of manuscript in double-spaced, word-processed pages, including references, figures, and appendices
- Assertion that the manuscript is unpublished and not submitted elsewhere
- Awards or grants associated with the manuscript
- Question or statement that demonstrates elements above, such as the purpose and unique nature of the manuscript, and knowledge of the journal

EXAMPLE: Journal Editor Query [Email]

Dear [Dr., Mr., Ms.] [First name, Last name]:

Good day. You may recall that we met briefly at the ALA Midwinter Meeting in San Diego. We were introduced by my Director, [First and last name]. I just completed work on a paper that I believe would be a good fit for [Journal name], and I wish gauge your interest. The paper, "[descriptive manuscript title]", is a case study on [topic]. A grant from [Funding agency] was used to collect data for assessing the impact of [topic]. Results demonstrate that [brief conclusions].

There is a paucity of case studies about [topic] in the literature that have the data to show these results. I know that [Journal name] commonly publishes case studies; two of them are cited in my paper. However, readers of this case will benefit from [distinguishing details].

My paper is [number] double-spaced pages in length, including references and appendices. It is not previously published, nor has it been submitted elsewhere. The complete abstract is below. Would you please be kind enough to indicate whether or not the paper is an appropriate submission for [Journal title]?

EXAMPLE: Journal Editor Query [Email] , cont.

[Abstract]

Thank you very much for your time and consideration. I look forward to hearing from you.

Sincerely,

[Name]
[Affiliation]
[Address and contact information]

Finally, authors should heed the manner and tone of an editor's reply to the query; this can be equally as informative as the content of the reply. Beyond addressing the specific questions in the query, an editor's reply should be collegial, courteous, professional, prompt, and welcoming. Editors who come across as abrasive, aloof, dismissive, harshly critical, tardy, terse, or otherwise unprofessional, or who give the impression that they simply cannot be bothered, are unworthy of authors' further time or consideration.

5

Elements of the Publishing Process

This chapter is devoted to requisite elements of the publishing process that often require advice, clarification, definition, or explanation. These elements include manuscript preparation, manuscript submission, peer review, editorial decisions, and manuscript revisions. Particular emphasis is given to these elements as they pertain to the publishing of scholarly papers. Although there is a modest amount of overlapping coverage, the authors of books and edited volumes will find more relevant discussion of the publishing process in the Scholarly Book section of the present text.

5.1 *Manuscript Preparation*

It borders on the obvious to assert the critical importance of different elements in the publishing process; they are all vitally important. However, the essential nature of finishing one's writing project by fully, completely, and appropriately preparing it for submission cannot be overemphasized. All of the effort that an author applies to his or her manuscript can be irreparably compromised by inadequate submission preparations, or by failing to follow proper procedures.

The natural inclination for many authors—having devoted so much time and effort to their writing—is to submit their work for review as quickly as possible. However, preparing one's work for submission requires a final push of diligence and patience. Diligence is needed to make certain that one's work is truly finished, polished, and appropriately formatted for an intended journal, and patience is needed to allow for at least one capable, knowledgeable, and trustworthy colleague to comb the manuscript in an effort to find anything that the author may have missed. Authors are encouraged to consult the following checklist in order to best prepare their scholarly work for submission. Although some of the listed recommendations will seem abundantly evident for many of the intended readers, the same readers would likely be shocked to discover the relatively high percentage of LIS authors who fail to follow through with simple, sensible, manuscript preparations.

- **Run spelling and grammar-checks.** The default settings for most of the familiar word processing applications include spell-check and grammar-check features that run continuously in the background. Still, authors commonly opt to disregard the "ignore," "ignore once," and "ignore all" suggestions of their word processing applications, or they switch off those automated correcting features altogether. It is understandable, particularly with lengthier manuscripts, that authors will sometimes forget about the numerous instances of grammar or spelling that they right-clicked on and ignored. It is also understandable that authors will sometimes forget to switch those checking features back on again when they are done writing. However, any text that is identified as potentially being erroneous should be double-checked. Automated correcting features are by no means perfect, but they do help to limit instances of poor mechanics that reflect so badly on an author's work.
- **Standardize manuscript format.** Most LIS publications require and expect the following standard formatting features:

  » Double-spaced text.
  » Flush left and ragged right justification. Never use flush left and flush right full justification. Center justification may be used for headings, subheadings, figures, and tables.
  » Indented new paragraphs. Use tab indentations instead of space bar indentations.
  » 1.00 inch top and bottom margins and 1.25 inch left and right margins. 1.00 inch left and right margins are commonly accepted.
  » Times New Roman font theme. Ariel and Calibri are commonly accepted. Other fonts will stand out as unusual, which can have a subtle impact on how editors and reviewers perceive the overall work.
  » 12 point font size. 11 point is commonly accepted. 10 point font may be used in figures and tables. Chicago Style endnote numbers and APA Style footnote numbers that appear in-text must be superscripted.

> » Automatic black font color; no text effects. Beware of relative inconsistencies that commonly occur when text is copied and pasted from other sources.
> » Single spaces between words, and also between punctuation and words (e.g., no double spaces between periods and the beginning of subsequent sentences).

- **Blind manuscript.** Failing to blind one's work in preparation for peer review is among the most common manuscript preparation mistakes. This problem became more prevalent as the nature of LIS work became more electronic, and as authors began producing papers with more widely identifiable information (e.g., file names, web addresses, computer screenshots, etc.). Another contributing factor is the advent of automated manuscript submission processes; authors fail to recognize or trust that their personal metadata will follow their work by virtue of authentication (i.e., username and password), and as such, they commonly leave their names atop title pages, the names of their institutions in abstracts, and so on. Authors must be scrupulous in their efforts to blind their work—thus preserving the integrity of the double-blind review process that is practiced with most LIS journals. The term "integrity" is essential to this point; reviewers are perfectly capable of searching across a familiar range of sources that can help them to identify manuscript authors if they are so inclined. However, LIS reviewers operate on a strict academic code of honor that precludes them from doing so or even from wanting to do so. Furthermore, the nature of LIS scholarship is such that virtually no manuscripts can be easily attributed to any one specific author (see Peer Review section). As a result, it is incumbent on authors to double-check their work for any information that can be directly associated with themselves or their co-authors, their institutions, or any related professional groups or projects. Particular attention should be paid to the following areas:

> » The file name.
> » The manuscript title page (Reminder: Journal management systems will automatically attribute necessary authorship to all manuscript submissions).

» Page headers and footers.
» In-text citations and endnote references.
» Figures, tables, and especially computer screenshots.
» The body of the manuscript (Note: Be certain to remove any identifiable institution or professional group names, descriptions, abbreviations, acronyms, or web addresses).

- *Remove automated endnotes and footnotes.* This rule is explicitly stated in the manuscript submission guidelines for most scholarly journals, and still it is among the most common manuscript preparation mistakes.
- *Check style and accuracy.* This recommendation cannot be overemphasized. An author's manuscript must conform to standards in the style manual or style sheet that is required by a publisher or a publication. The nature of LIS requires bibliographic and stylistic accuracy and precision, and because editors and reviewers are peers in the profession, they have little tolerance for the inaccurate and the imprecise. Fair or not, inconsistently or incorrectly formatted manuscripts can be rejected outright, regardless of the subject matter. The most commonly identified style errors occur when authors do the following :

  » Fail to consult, understand, or abide by the required standards and conventions in a required style manual or style sheet.
  » Switch between styles (Note: This tends to occur when authors have their submitted work rejected by one publication, and then they resubmit elsewhere).
  » Copy and paste unformatted citations from online bibliographic sources.
  » Fail to double-check the accuracy of citations imported from bibliographic management software programs (e.g., *EndNote* or *Zotero*).

- *Check figures and tables.* The familiar style manuals for LIS authors include details for creating, formatting, and referring to figures and tables. Likewise, publishers and individual publications usually have their own specifications, often requiring that figures and tables be provided as separate documents. Authors must take care to abide by such requirements; they must also make certain that manuscript figures and tables are presented consistently in terms of:

- » Design.
- » Character conventions (i.e., font and punctuation).
- » Linguistic conventions (i.e., vocabulary and phraseology).
- » Placement within the text (e.g., "<Table 2 here>").
- » Reference within the text (e.g., "…as shown in Figure 2").
- » Proper alphanumeric order.

- *Check subheadings.* The nature of the writing process commonly requires that authors reorganize their work for the purpose of creating a more logical flow. As this reorganization takes place, the relevance of initial subheadings may vary, their alphanumeric order or design conventions may change, or the creation of new ones may become necessary. Authors are encouraged to double-check subheadings for consistency, order, and relevance.
- *Check references.* Cited sources must be impeccably accurate. The most commonly identified errors related to references occur when authors do the following :

  - » Fail to give appropriate credit for previous work.
  - » Fail to blind any references to an author's own previous works.
  - » Fail to format in-text or endnote references according to the required style manual or style sheet.
  - » Mismatch different citation styles.
  - » Misspell cited authors' names, or spell them differently in-text and then in the endnote references.
  - » Provide inaccurate information (Note: Authors should pay particular attention to publication and access dates, volume and issue numbers, web addresses, and digital object identifiers).

- *Switch off automated editing features* (e.g., the Track Changes feature in *Microsoft Word*).

- ***Take time off.*** The crafting of a scholarly paper requires constant revision. The more times an author reads over the same sentences, passages, or paragraphs, the more likely that he or she will miss subtle, or even obvious errors in flow, logic, and mechanics. While it is true that a hard push of diligence is required to fully prepare a manuscript for submission, it is also true that a rested and refreshed author will catch and correct more writing errors. Authors are highly encouraged to take a day or more away from their manuscript in order to recharge, and to spend that time focused on other matters.
- ***Proofread.*** Once refreshed, authors are encouraged to proofread their work once more. As noted throughout the course of this text, reading one's work aloud is a particularly effective method for detecting errors.
- ***Have a colleague review.*** Selecting an appropriate colleague to review one's work is vitally important, and if possible, authors are recommended to have more than one colleague review their work. Another LIS professional's perspective is necessary for making certain that one's work is effectively argued and presented, and also for catching errors in flow, logic, and mechanics that an author may have overlooked. The colleague selected should be an experienced author, a skilled writer and editor, and an honest reviewer (i.e., willing to provide all necessary criticisms). Additionally, that person should be knowledgeable about the subject matter of an author's manuscript, and he or she should be well-versed in the related professional literature.
- ***Synthesize comments and criticisms.*** Having a colleague review one's manuscript is a useful practice run for having that work undergo the formal the peer-review process. Authors are encouraged to be gracious and professional with colleague reviewers, and to genuinely consider their comments and criticisms without regarding any of them as personal attacks.
- ***Edit, revise, and proofread again.*** After fully considering their colleagues' comments and criticisms, authors should make the changes they deem to be necessary for the betterment of their work. Even the most experienced and polished LIS authors will need to revise their work, particularly at this early stage of the publishing process. Although

manuscript fatigue is common and understandable at this point, authors are again encouraged to let their revised manuscript sit for a day or more before one last proofreading.

5.2 *Manuscript Submission*

As a reminder, the focus of this chapter is on publishing scholarly papers. Submission processes can be significantly different for non-refereed periodicals or for non-periodical publications. Scholarly journals will have specific, and often quite exacting requirements for manuscript submissions. These are consistently detailed in the author guidelines area of a journal's web site, or in the front or back matter of its print edition. Author guidelines will include explicit requirements for manuscript preparations—often with useful examples—and the necessary procedures for submitting one's work. Even with these readily available guidelines, LIS authors commonly and surprisingly fail to abide by one or more of them.

Electronic vs. Print Submission. Most scholarly LIS journals require electronic submissions either by way of sending manuscripts as email attachments to the editor, by using free web transfer applications like *Dropbox* (available at https://www.dropbox.com), or by uploading them through an automated journal management system. A small number of journals still obdurately require multiple print copies of manuscripts to be sent through the mail, and a small number of those actually require both print and electronic submissions; these particular publications represent a quickly diminishing minority among LIS journals, and they risk becoming irrelevant. As such, these publications are given little attention in this section of the text.

Email Submission. Author responsibilities are reasonably clear for journals that require submissions by way of email attachments. If a manuscript is properly prepared according to the publisher or publication guidelines, then simply attaching it to an email message addressed to the editor is an easy final step. Importantly, this submission method affords authors the opportunity to include a cover letter in the body of the email message (see

Cover Letter section). It also allows authors to easily and efficiently keep records of their publication-related correspondences. When submitting their work, authors are encouraged to ask corresponding editors to confirm that they have received all the necessary file attachments, and also that there are no complications with opening or reading those files.

Automated Submission. An ever-increasing number of LIS journal publishers are adopting or developing their own automated journal management systems. Among other necessary functions that are discussed in the Journal Management Systems section, these automated programs include step-by-step instructions for manuscript submissions. Typically, authors are required to begin by creating an account with a username and password, and then they are permitted to commence with the necessary procedures for submitting their work. As authors are led through the automated submission process, they are instructed to provide information about their manuscript in order to assist editors with managing the journal's work flow. Beyond requisite information like the manuscript's title, abstract, keywords, and length, authors are commonly asked to indicate the type of submission (e.g., research paper or case study), and to describe the work's purpose, design, implications, and overall value to the professional literature. Authors may be asked to disclose funding sources, affirm the necessary approval of any human subject-related research, or declare that no part of the manuscript is submitted elsewhere for publication. In practical terms, this is the automated version of an author's cover message (see Cover Message to Editor section). Authors may also be asked at this point to approve or electronically sign a journal-specific statement of copyright (see Copyright section). The final step of the submission process involves uploading one's work to a journal's web site; this will generate an automated email message that is sent to both the author and the editor, which confirms receipt of the manuscript and triggers the next steps toward publication.

Journal Management Systems

Journal management systems are developed and used to improve overall journal work flow and efficiency through sophisticated, online automation processes. For electronic-only journals, these systems are often part of the production process, too. Commercial and open access publishers are the profession's earliest adopters and developers of journal management systems, but all types of LIS publishers will inevitably follow suit. Larger commercial publishers typically have more money and staffing to devote to developing their own journal management systems—for example, Elsevier's *Elsevier Editorial System* (EES), which was launched in 2002 (Elsevier, 2012). Comparatively smaller commercial LIS publishers trend toward adopting existing journal management systems—for example, Emerald's adoption of Thomson Scientific's *ScholarOne* product in 2007 (Thomson Reuters, 2007). Open access publishers characteristically adopt existing open source journal management programs, and by far, *Open Journal Systems* (OJS) is the most commonly used. The OJS program was "developed by the Public Knowledge Project through its federally funded efforts to expand and improve access to research" (Public Knowledge Project, 2012). Examples of scholarly LIS journals that are published on the OJS platform include *Communications in Information Literacy, Evidence Based Library and Information Practice, Journal of Library Innovation, Library and Information Research*, and *Library Student Journal*.

Journal management systems are designed for and used by all of the relevant parties of a scholarly journal: authors, editors, reviewers, copyeditors, and in the instance of some electronic-only journals, even the readers. The interface and the automated functions that are designed for each of these parties will differ based on their particular role in the publication process, but all of the functions are interdependent and systematically coordinated. The most pertinent functions for authors are manuscript preparation, submission, peer review, and the editorial decision. Based on the editorial decision, subsequent automated functions may include revisions, copyedits, and the proofing of galleys. These are the same functions and processes that have always been in place with scholarly journals; the only differences are the medium and the administrative methods.

Authors should know that automation does not remove the human factor from the overall process; very human journal editors remain in control, and very human reviewers still provide the necessary criticisms and feedback. Journal management systems are not perfect, but when they are developed, implemented, and used properly, they can improve the overall publication process substantially. The most common journal management system problems that occur are technical in nature. Authors working with these systems can mitigate or even avoid most technical problems by simply following a given journal's web site browser specifications, and also by checking their email account spam filters to make certain that automated messages concerning their work are not blocked.

Cover Message to Editor

The evolution of the manuscript submission process from print-and-mail to point-and-click has had an impact on the fashioning and overall use of cover messages. The former art of crafting an effective cover letter to an editor is largely distilled down to an accompanying email message, and with the advent of automated journal management systems, the so-called cover message is sometimes subdivided into a small number of lifeless, character-limited text fields. Still, the importance of providing an effective and well-written cover message is critical; it continues the line of communication that was generated by way of the original query (see Querying Journal Editors section), it serves to advance a favorable relationship with the journal editor, and it helps the editor to plan subsequent actions, such as selecting appropriate manuscript reviewers.

The cover message should be a follow-up to the editor query; in many respects, it is a reminder or a reiteration of the information in that original message. As asserted in the Querying Journal Editors section, authors should always make it as easy as possible for editors to do their work. In terms of the cover message, it should be professional, but above all things, it should be succinct. Almost all LIS journal editors conduct their business through email; this makes the provision of a cover message easy when manuscript submission is required by way of an email attachment. In the instance of manuscript submission by way of an automated journal management system, authors should try their best to include all of the necessary elements listed below in required text fields:

- Reminder of previous correspondence related to the manuscript.
- Brief description of the purpose and unique nature of the manuscript.
- Reminder of why the manuscript is an appropriate fit for the journal.

- Manuscript title and abstract.
- Length of manuscript in double-spaced, word-processed pages, including references, figures, tables, appendices, and word count.
- Assertion that the manuscript is unpublished and not submitted elsewhere.
- Avowal of any necessary copyright permissions or human subject-related approvals.
- Awards or grants associated with the manuscript.
- Request for confirmation that the manuscript is received, and also that there are no complications with opening or reading the submission files (Note: With journal management systems, the confirmation email message is automatically generated and sent to the author).

EXAMPLE: Cover Message to Editor

Dear [Dr., Mr., Ms.] [First name, Last name]:

Good day. In response to your kind encouragement in our previous email exchange, I am submitting my manuscript, "[Title]," for possible publication in [Journal name]. The manuscript is [number] double-spaced pages and [number] words in length, including references and appendices. No part of this work is previously published or submitted elsewhere; all necessary permissions are granted and fully documented. For your convenience, I included the complete abstract at the end of this message.

As a reminder, the attached manuscript is a case study on [topic]. A grant from [Funding agency] was used to collect data for assessing the impact of [topic], and results demonstrate that [brief conclusions]. I know that [Journal name] commonly publishes case studies; two of them are cited in my paper. However, readers of this case will benefit from [distinguishing details].

Would you please be kind enough to confirm receipt of this manuscript, and also to confirm that there are no complications with opening the file? Thank you very much for your time and consideration. I look forward to hearing from you.

Sincerely,

[Name]
[Affiliation]
[Address and contact information]

[Title]
[Abstract]

5.3 Peer Review

As discussed in multiple sections of the present text, most scholarly LIS journals are peer-reviewed, which is synonymous with the terms refereed and juried. All of these terms refer to a process by which manuscripts are submitted to a scholarly journal, and then distributed to subject experts on a review or editorial board for evaluation and commentary. The subject experts, who are peers in the profession or in a particular area of study, serve as manuscript reviewers, referees, and jurors; thus the terms peer-reviewed, refereed, and juried. Critical to the integrity of this process, information that might potentially identify reviewers or individual authors and their institutions is removed from manuscripts prior to review; thus the related term "blind-reviewed."

Single vs. Double-Blind Review

There is an ongoing, passionate debate concerning use and value of the peer review process in the greater community of researchers and scholars, but more recently there is a particular reexamination of the pros and cons of single versus double-blind peer review. Single-blind refers to a practice by which the identities of manuscript reviewers are removed from the review process, but authors' names and institutional affiliations remain. Double-blind refers to a practice by which the identities of reviewers, authors, and institutions are all removed from the review process. Although this debate is not entirely a new one, it is more recently intensified by the possibilities that scholars recognize in the web-based environment, and also by the resulting, profound changes in the world of scholarly communication.

Many scholars contend that it is increasingly difficult to maintain a viable double-blind system of review; their contentions are both practical and philosophical in nature. To begin, well-read and well-informed scholars argue that they can often recognize the signature arguments, methods, research topics, and even the writing styles of peers within their narrow fields of expertise, and in such circumstances, double-blinding is a significant challenge. Equally, some scholars assert that the capability of searching across a familiar range of subscription-based and free web sources provides reviewers, if they are so inclined, with the opportunity to identify manuscript authors with relative ease. Although these matters are deserving of some consideration, they are not particularly concerning to the scholarly LIS community. Pritchard (2012) wrote eloquently on this point:

> In the vigorous pro and con debate over these ideas and practices there is some unnecessary conflation of terms and polarization of options. One can have open access publishing, for example, and still retain double-blind peer preview. Open review, and crowd-sourcing, can be set up so that only an editor sees all the identities, or so that final decisions are still made up by a selective appointed editorial board. (p. 117)

Perhaps a more compelling argument for single-blind and against double-blind reviewing lies in the emergence of an open access and open source culture in which there are expectations of fewer barriers and more transparency, even in the area of scholarly communication. The implications of this new culture are both profound and wide-ranging; scholars are generally more accommodating to new forms of collaborative authorship (e.g., wikis), and they are more accepting of commentary and criticism that may come by way of free web-based communications (e.g., weblogs). The impact of these changes is equally profound and wide-ranging for the scholarly publishing industry. Commercial publishers, in particular, are being forced to adapt to increased demands for open access models—although their solutions are often regressive and cynical. Publishers are also being pressed for more benign and flexible copyright permissions that allow for authors to independently post reprints online or to include them in institutional repositories.

The ongoing debate over the practicality and viability of single versus double-blind reviewing varies in intensity among the academic disciplines, and as demonstrated by Souder's review of the literature (2010), there is no shortage of professional discourse devoted to the topic. Ultimately, however, the issue of bias trumps most arguments. Even if one assumes the very best of professional intentions in manuscript reviewers, they are still human and they have inherent biases. The slightest subconscious trace of bias related to an author's gender, ideology, institutional affiliation, nationality, or even his or her previous works can potentially have an impact on the way in which reviewers process a manuscript submission. As evidence of this, Budden, et al. (2008) showed that the practice of double-blind reviewing increases the likelihood of manuscript submissions by women, and Ross, et al. (2006) demonstrated that double-blinding reduces biases relative to nationality and institutional affiliation. Even more compellingly, Laband and Piette (1994) conducted a study demonstrating that when reviewers know author identities, they employ more particular criteria for evaluating manuscripts, and as a result, "…journals using nonblinded peer review publish a larger fraction of papers that should not have been published than do journals using blinded peer review" (p. 147). Furthermore, the authors of this particular study showed that, "Articles published in journals using blinded peer review were cited significantly more than articles published in journals using nonblinded peer review" (p. 147). Although Laband and Piette's study did not include LIS journals, their conclusions are applicable to the review process for all disciplines, and they reinforce a widely held notion in the LIS community that double-blind peer review continues to be an important criterion in terms of overall journal impact and quality.

Peer Review and LIS Journals

The peer review process is not a perfect one for any discipline. Via (1996) found evidence of inconsistent review practices among a significant sample of LIS journals. However, the intended audience for this text should be reassured that the community of LIS journal editors is exceptionally well-informed in terms of the evolving nature of peer review, the relative controversies, and ultimately, the best practices. As a result, most LIS journals continue to practice double-blind peer review. At the 2008 American Library Association's Midwinter Meeting, a meeting of leading, independent LIS editors was convened to "discuss common concerns and identify practices that can strengthen the collective ability of the journals to serve the discipline and the professionals who create and apply that literature" (Library and Information Science Editors, 2012). This group, now known officially as the LIS Editors, developed a "Guide to Best Practices for Editors of Library and Information Science Journals" (2009), which outlines and promotes standard editorial ethics and best editorial practices in the discipline. As noted by Pritchard (2012), this guide does not mandate the use of double-blind review, but "it encourages some form of peer review and outlines the level of openness and procedural care that each journal should take in explaining its mission and determining its forms of review" (p. 119). All authors are encouraged to consult this thoughtful guide.

Manuscript Review Process

The most common model of peer review involves a sequence of work flow procedures that commence with an author's manuscript submission. The sequence is advanced by editorial administration and reviewer evaluation, and ultimately, it is concluded by an editorial decision to either accept or reject the manuscript (see Figure 1).

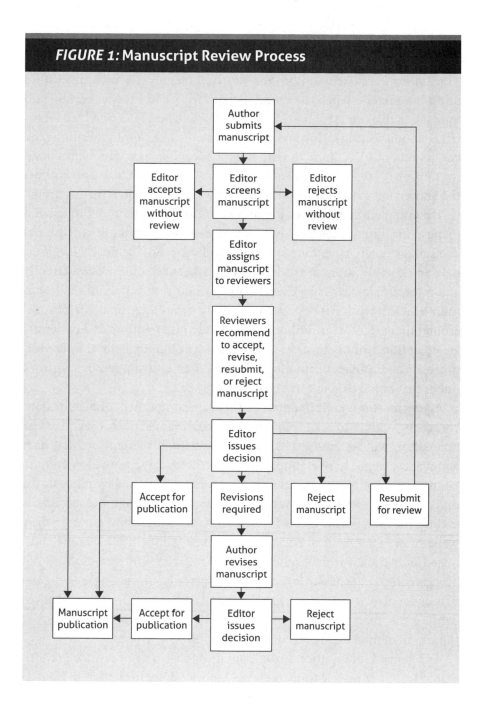

FIGURE 1: Manuscript Review Process

Manuscript Turnaround Time. The length of time between the manuscript submission and the editorial decision depends on numerous mitigating factors. Authors are likely to learn the decision quickly—sometimes within one or two days—when their work is not forwarded for peer review, and more often than not, that particular decision will be a rejection (see Editorial Decision section). However, there is an unspoken protocol among the community of LIS editors to wait at least a few business days before issuing this type of rejection; true or not, editors believe that this gives authors the impression that greater consideration was given to their manuscripts.

The complete sequence of procedural steps that is required to usher a manuscript through the peer review process and to arrive at an editorial decision generally takes four to twelve weeks for most scholarly LIS journals. Some publications are consistently quicker and some are consistently and painfully slower. As a general statement on the matter, journals with more efficient work flow operations tend to have faster manuscript turnaround times. However, authors are reminded that editors and reviewers are exceptionally busy professionals, and more often than not they are volunteers; the business of running a journal is often trumped by the work duties that one is paid to carry out on a daily basis.

Asking for Manuscript Updates. Authors are sometimes conflicted about contacting editors to ask for updates on their manuscripts; they may fear that editors will be annoyed by such queries, and by extension, that such annoyances might have an impact on the editorial decision. However, no editor worthy of his or her title should ever feel bothered by requests for updates, and they should never give that ugly impression. Most journals include the average turnaround times for manuscript submissions on their web site or in the front or back matter of their print editions. Some automated journal management systems even allow for authors to track the developments of activities related to their manuscripts online, including the progress of individual reviewers. Furthermore, many editors will contact authors to confirm that their manuscripts have been sent for review, and to estimate the length of time before an editorial decision will be issued.

As a general rule, authors are encouraged to allow for the stated or estimated length of review time to elapse before asking for updates. There is an important exception to this rule; authors who are undergoing institutional review for contract renewal, appointment, promotion, or tenure should feel no reticence in asking editors for updates at any time, or even for letters confirming that their works are currently under consideration for possible publication. Editors understand these dynamics very well, and they are highly supportive of their peers in the profession. If inquiries go unanswered, then authors are perfectly within their rights to withdraw their work from consideration. Manuscript submission is not a contract, and authors maintain full ownership of their work at this stage of the process. The unresponsive editor is usually a symptom of larger problem with a journal, and authors may be better served by submitting their work elsewhere.

Role of the Editor

Editors are typically experts in both the business of scholarly communication and in the subject matter that is particular to the journals for which they serve. Their primary responsibilities are to manage journal work flow, issue manuscript decisions, and communicate effectively with authors, reviewers, readers, and publishers. As their title suggests, editors are also responsible for the fine-grained work of editing manuscripts, and with some publications, they are involved in the production process as well. To the uninitiated, these responsibilities may seem clear and simple, but the role of editors is highly complex. At any given time, editors may need to use varying measures of decisiveness, diplomacy, professionalism, subtlety, and tactfulness in order to accomplish necessary tasks and to balance the interests of all relevant parties. Consider, for instance, the task of having to remove a reviewer from an editorial board because of his substandard evaluations or apparent partiality, or having to inform an author that her submitted work is being rejected when it is common knowledge that the author needs that publication for her tenure dossier. These are not uncommon scenarios, and they are only a small sampling of the many challenges that commonly face journal editors.

Editors must be attentive to the business of their journals, especially with respect to work flow; their ability to keep authors and reviewers on task is critical for maintaining a regular publication schedule. This is a vital concern to publishers, because a consistent, reliable publication schedule is an important factor in maintaining a journal's reputation. To varying degrees, editors are also responsible for marketing their journals, and in some instances, they conduct the business of getting those publications indexed. Editors also communicate to their readership with calls for papers, announcements of new or special issues, and pronouncements relative to their journals or to developments in their fields of practice or research.

Journal editors are often responsible for recruiting and appointing manuscript reviewers. This has a direct and immediate impact on journal operations and reputations. Reliable and effective reviewers are necessary for journal efficiency and quality, and the presence of widely recognizable reviewers is necessary for imbuing author confidence and building journal prestige. Editors must also be scrupulous in protecting the integrity of the peer review process, watching for possible instances of partiality, and guarding against any real or perceived conflicts of interest. These particular issues are less concerning in LIS than they are with other disciplines, but editorial vigilance remains as an essential ingredient to the business of publishing scholarly papers.

Editors have a great familiarity with their professional literature, and that familiarity extends to a point of personal or professional acquaintance with many scholars. Editors know what has been accomplished in their field, and by whom, and they have an informed vision for what remains to be done. As a result, editors are in a position of authority that permits the soliciting of manuscripts from desirable authors. Given their disciplinary knowledge and vision, editors are also qualified to weigh the evaluations of peer reviewers and to pass editorial judgment on submitted works.

Traditionally, journal editors were eminent figures in their particular fields of research or practice. To a large degree, this continues to be true for editors of many LIS publications. However, comparatively new developments in the profession and in the business of scholarly communication have occasioned some changes that relate to journal editors' overall notoriety. The recent upsurge in scholarly LIS productivity, the dramatic proliferation of new LIS journals, and in particular, the possibilities of web-based and open access publishing have contributed to a rapidly expanding disciplinary literature in which it is more accurate to suggest that editors are generally known to their peers. In simple terms, there are many new editors, and not all of them are well-known in the profession. This does not diminish their importance, their work, or the high regard that LIS professionals have for journal editors in general; it is simply a matter of recognition. Library and information science editors will continue to earn the reputation and status that they deserve the old-fashioned way—by virtue of their overall contributions to the literature and to the discipline.

Role of the Reviewer

Manuscript reviewers are qualified authorities in the subject matter that is particular to the journals for which they serve. Most often reviewers are educators, practitioners, researchers, or specialists from institutions that are external to the publishers of those journals. In simple terms, the role of reviewers is to use their knowledge and experience in particular areas of research or practice in order to evaluate manuscript submissions as potential contributions to the journals for which they serve, and by extension, for the greater body of LIS literature. It is the reviewers' responsibility to judge the overall quality of submitted works in terms of relevance, scholarship, timeliness, noteworthiness, and even the writing style, and then to provide editors with written evaluations. Reviewer evaluations generally include their analyses, critical remarks, suggested changes, and recommendations for editorial decisions (see Manuscript Decisions section). More often than not, reviewer evaluations, or modified versions of them, are also shared with contributing authors when editorial decisions are issued for their work.

Reviewer Appointment. Manuscript reviewers are commonly recruited and appointed to review boards by journal editors. Recruitment is based primarily on the reviewers' subject area knowledge, but manuscript evaluation experience is clearly another important consideration. Most LIS editors have the authority to appoint reviewers, but appointments are sometimes subject to approval from existing board members. Reviewers can also be recruited on the basis of their professional reputation; editors will unabashedly leverage reviewers' standing in the profession for the purpose of bolstering a journal's authority, credibility, and prestige. Reviewers may also be unsolicited volunteers, or they may come to a journal in response to an editor's open call for new reviewers. Reviewers who volunteer in one manner or another are ordinarily asked to show by way of their professional dossier that they have the necessary subject area knowledge. If volunteers have the subject knowledge, but lack the desired manuscript evaluation experience, editors will generally compensate by teaming them with more experienced reviewers when the time comes for manuscript assignments.

Reviewer Motivation. There are numerous personal and professional motivations for becoming a manuscript reviewer, including sincere interest and investment in the subject matter, desire to contribute to the profession, and the more practical need to demonstrate professional service in one's academic dossier. Reviewers may feel obligated to serve for a particular editor or publisher, they may enjoy a sense of accomplishment that comes with their work, and they may even experience an elevated sense of stature. In a comparatively dated work, however, Bauer (1984) proposed that there are also more cynical motivations for serving as a manuscript reviewer. The author suggested that reviewers may use their position to lambaste their professional competition, to delay publication of competing works, or even to plagiarize (p. 33). Fortunately, there is no evidence to indicate that these disturbing propositions are applicable to LIS reviewers.

Reviewer Selection. Matching reviewers with manuscript submissions is most commonly accomplished by way of a volunteer model or an assignment model. With the volunteer model, reviewer boards are alerted by editors that manuscripts have been submitted, and then individual reviewers can volunteer to evaluate them based on their own availability or interest in those works. More often, however, reviewers are assigned to manuscript submissions by a journal editor. Manuscript assignments are typically based on a combination of factors, including basic rotation within a journal's pool of reviewers, and the matching of individual reviewers' research interests or expertise to the subject matter of individual submissions. Some journals have internal rating scales for ranking their reviewers, or even different tiers that are based on experience or the quality of previous reviews. Internal procedures for a journal may require that any given manuscript has at least one advanced level or proven reviewer to ensure a necessary measure of quality control. This is particularly important for instances in which reviewer evaluations include differing recommendations. Editors will typically give greater consideration to the advanced level or proven reviewer's comments and suggestions, and they will sometimes indicate that factor when issuing a manuscript decision.

Reviewer Guidelines. The practices of most LIS journals require that reviewers base their manuscript evaluations on specific criteria or detailed evaluation guidelines that are developed and provided by editors or publishers. Although contributing authors can sometimes gauge those criteria or guidelines through a close reading of the content, format, and organization of manuscript evaluations, specific reviewer criteria documents are rarely shared by editors. For the purpose of showing the intended readers of this text a sample of the criteria by which reviewers generally evaluate manuscripts, the guidelines used by reviewers for the journal, *Communications in information Literacy* (Goosney & Hollister, 2009), are appended to the end of this chapter (see Appendix 1).

Manuscript Mentoring. Only a few LIS journals provide one form or another of mentoring to encourage scholarly contributions from relatively new, inexperienced, or international authors. There are two models of journal-provided author mentoring: pre- review and post-review. For the pre-review model, journal editors typically solicit volunteers from their pool of reviewers to serve as mentors; those volunteers are paired with mentee authors after the original editorial screenings of manuscript submissions. The purpose of mentoring prior to peer review is to best prepare submitted works for the review process; editors will select volunteers based on a rotation queue, or on the reviewers' availability, area expertise, research interests, language skills, or mentoring abilities. Post-review mentoring can be a challenge; editors must be certain to protect the integrity of the double-blind review process. As it follows, mentors must be selected from outside the original group of reviewers that were assigned to an author's manuscript. Sometimes the editor, him or herself, will serve as a mentor, using reviewers' evaluations to inform the nature of necessary mentorship. It should be noted, however, that editors often lack the time to serve in this dual capacity; thus, the need for additional volunteers.

Library and information science authors—particularly those who are inexperienced or who are non-native English speakers—are encouraged to seek out journals that provide mentoring services, but they should know that those publications are few and far between. Authors may include questions about the availability of mentoring services, or about related policies and procedures in their query messages to journal editors (see Querying Journal Editors section). Publications that offer mentoring will likely boast of the service on their web sites or in the front or back matter of their print editions. As an example, the author guidelines for *Library Resources and Technical Services* (2012) include the following language:

> The editor and editorial board are committed to assisting authors to produce publishable papers. If a paper shows promise, but needs more work, and the author wishes to work with a mentor, the editor will pair the author with someone (usually a member of the editorial board) who can help the author with revisions. (para. 8)

It is noteworthy that most LIS journals would prefer to include mentoring if they had the necessary staffing, and if there was a proven link between the provision of that service and manuscripts ultimately being accepted for publication. Unfortunately, the former of these conditions is rarely true, and the latter is not shown to be true. For several years, mentoring was a hallmark service provided by the prestigious journal, *portal: Libraries and the Academy*. However, that service was discontinued due to the aforementioned matters of practicality and diminished returns, and also by the reality that generating and sustaining long-distance mentoring relationships between unacquainted professionals is a significant challenge. As if speaking for the community of LIS journal editors, the editor of *portal* (2012) encourages mentorship, but puts the responsibility on authors to seek that valuable, professional guidance on their own:

> All submissions to *portal* are subjected to the double-blind review process, and referees are explicitly asked to indicate when a manuscript is worthy but needs more detailed guidance in order to be fully acceptable for publication in *portal*. When a recommendation is made to find a mentor for a manuscript, the author is asked if they wish to undertake such an effort, understanding that the process is up to them to carry forward. (para. 10)

5.4 *Manuscript Decisions*

Without Peer Review: Accept or Reject Manuscript

Referring to Figure 1, one can see that manuscript submissions are sometimes accepted or rejected prior to peer review. Manuscripts accepted prior to the review process are usually solicited works; more often than not they are published as editorials and perspectives pieces, and by definition, they are non-refereed (see Type of Articles section). It is far more common, however, for an editor to issue a rejection than an acceptance at this point of the process. Most journal editors practice a form of editorial triage in which they screen manuscript submissions prior to sending them for review in order to make certain that those works are appropriate for their journal. Manuscripts deemed to be significantly unprofessional, unscholarly, inappropriate, or deficient in some other way can be, and sometimes are rejected without being sent for review.

Rejection without peer review happens for many reasons. To begin, editors are highly sensitive about wasting their reviewers' valuable time and expertise on submissions that stand virtually no chance of surviving the review process. Editors are also mindful of protecting the integrity and prestige of their journal by ushering through only those manuscripts that have the potential to be unique and useful contributions to the literature. Finally, editors rarely have the available time or staffing that is required for improving poorly developed or badly written manuscripts; this is increasingly the case for works that are submitted by authors from non-English speaking countries. The possibilities of today's Internet-based communications have resulted in a dramatic rise in the numbers of international LIS manuscript submissions, and though LIS publishers welcome and highly encourage them, the development of the subject matter and the quality of writing in those works are sometimes beyond the help that editors can realistically provide.

When editors issue rejection notices for manuscripts that were not forwarded for review, they are unlikely to include any reporting of that particular detail. This is a tactful omission; editors are heedful that the inclusion of such information may offend contributing authors. In their communications with authors, editors strive to achieve a balance between a necessary professionalism that can sometimes be perceived by authors as harsh, and a desired gentleness that is intended to leave an overall positive impression of the journal. The rejection-without-review notice may include brief, encouraging remarks, or even suggestions about other, more relevant publication venues. Ultimately, however, when editors issue this type of notice, they will clearly and unambiguously state that the manuscript is rejected.

EXAMPLE: Notice of Manuscript Rejection without Review

Dear [Authors(s)]...

Thank you for your recent manuscript submission, "[Manuscript title]," to [Journal name]. You present an interesting study on the effects of [subject matter]. However, after careful consideration, we have determined that your work does not fit the current needs of this journal. The editors believe that [brief, general reasons for rejection, and/or distantly encouraging remarks].

Thank you again for submitting your scholarly work to [Journal name]. Please feel free to contact us with any questions or concerns. We look forward to hearing from you again in the future.

Best regards,

[Editor]
[Contact information]

With Peer Review: Accept, Revise, Resubmit, or Reject Manuscript

Accept for Publication. When a manuscript is accepted for publication, the editor will typically commence with a welcoming, congratulatory note, and then follow with an indication of when the paper will be published, including the projected journal volume and issue numbers. Sometimes the editor will issue this notice as a conditional acceptance, assuming that the author will be amenable to making minor adjustments, and that he or she will be able to complete them in a timely manner. The conditional acceptance notice will include a list of recommended revisions, sometimes presented by way of the reviewers' original comments, and sometimes collected and organized by the editor to facilitate easier understanding. Even elegantly written, polished, and well-argued papers that are crafted by experienced and skilled authors will often require at least a small number of revisions. Although they are necessary, such revisions will not be of a significant nature; otherwise, the manuscript would not have been accepted. The conditional acceptance notice will also include a deadline for completing the revisions and instructions for returning the final version of the manuscript to the editor. Finally, if it was not a necessary procedure during the original submission process, the acceptance notice may also include instructions for signing a publisher's memorandum of agreement or copyright permissions statement (see Copyright section).

EXAMPLE: Notice of Manuscript Acceptance

Dear [Author(s)]...

I am pleased to report that your manuscript, "[Article title]," has been accepted for publication in [Journal name]. Congratulations! Your work will appear as a feature article in volume [number], issue [number], which is scheduled for publication in [month/season and year]. I will

---

EXAMPLE: Notice of Manuscript Acceptance, cont.

contact you when the time comes for final copyedits and for proofing the galleys. Until that time, please print out the attached [publisher agreement and/or copyright permission form], complete the [areas of the form] and sign it, and then return it to me by way of the fax number below or as an email attachment. I will need to have this completed form by [date]. If you have any questions or concerns, please feel free to contact me. Congratulations again, and thank you for contributing your scholarly work to [Journal name].

Sincerely,

[Editor]
[Title, address, contact information]

EXAMPLE: Conditional Notice of Manuscript Acceptance

Dear [Author(s)]...

I am pleased to report that your manuscript, "[Article title]," has been conditionally accepted for publication in [Journal name]. Congratulations! Assuming that you will be willing and able to make some modest, but necessary revisions, your work will appear as a feature article in volume [number], issue [number], which is scheduled for publication in [month/season and year].

As you will see in the attached reviewer evaluations document, your manuscript was very well received. However, the reviewers found that [minor manuscript shortcomings]. Additionally, they provided some useful recommendations for improving [other minor shortcomings]. Please read over the suggested changes that are outlined by the reviewers, with particular attention to [editor's input], make the necessary revisions, and then return the final draft to me as an email attachment. The deadline for returning the final draft to me is [date]. Please let me know if disagree with any of the suggested changes, or if you require more time.

Additionally, please print out the attached [publisher agreement and/or copyright permission form], complete the [areas of the form] and sign it, and then return it to me by way of the fax number below or as an email attachment. I will need to have this completed form by [date].

If you have any questions or concerns, please feel free to contact me. Congratulations again, and thank you for contributing your scholarly work to [Journal name].

Sincerely,

[Editor]
[Title, address, contact information]

Revisions Required. When an editor issues a "revisions required" decision, he or she is indicating to the author that one of two possible conditions are present. The first possibility is that specific manuscript changes must be in place in order for the editor to properly judge the work, and then to issue a final decision. The other possibility is that, with specified changes, the manuscript will be accepted for publication. The latter of these possible conditions is more common, but most LIS journal editors use the revisions required decision under both circumstances.

The revisions required notice will include a list of necessary changes, often presented by way of the reviewers' original comments, and sometimes collected and organized by the editor to facilitate easier understanding. The editor may also impress upon the author that some changes are more important than others. The necessary changes will be of a significant enough nature to preclude a final editorial decision, but those changes will not be significant enough to warrant a resubmit for review notice. The revisions required notice will often include a deadline for completing the necessary changes and returning the manuscript to the editor, particularly if that editor has a specific volume and issue in mind for possible publication. Editors may also ask that authors provide a supplemental document, along with the revised manuscript, detailing the changes they made, and also explaining their rationale for reviewer-recommended changes that they did not make.

EXAMPLE: Notice that Manuscript Revisions are Required

Dear [Author(s)]...

The review process for your manuscript, "[Manuscript title]," is completed, and the evaluations are attached to this message. As you will see, your manuscript has been well received, though it requires some revisions before we can make a final determination. Each reviewer would like to see some important changes to the paper, and there is considerable uniformity in their recommendations. Details of the necessary revisions are highlighted in the attached evaluations.

We ask that you please read and consider the attached evaluations, with particular attention to recommendations provided reviewers A and C. We believe that a heavier focus on... [editors' input]. If you are in agreement and wish to proceed with the revisions, we ask that you return the final draft to us as an email attachment by [date]. Once

Once we receive the revised manuscript, we can very quickly make a final determination. Also, we ask that you please include a separate, brief memo outlining how and why you did or did not address the reviewers' specific recommendations.

We look forward to reading your revised manuscript. Please feel free to contact us with any questions or concerns.

Sincerely,

[Editors]
[Address and contact information]

Resubmit for Review. The "resubmit for review" notice indicates to an author that his or her manuscript submission requires changes of a significant nature, but that the editor believes the work, or elements of it are potentially salvageable. The required changes, if carried out by the author, will result in a work that is considerably different from the original submission, and as such, it will need to undergo the peer review process once again.

The resubmit for review notice will include a substantial list of necessary changes, often presented by way of the reviewers' original comments, and sometimes collected and organized by the editor to facilitate easier understanding. The editor may attempt to encourage the author by emphasizing useful elements of the manuscript, but most of the notice will involve highly critical commentary and evaluation. The resubmit for review notice will rarely include a deadline for completing the necessary changes and then resubmitting, unless the editor has a specific volume and issue in mind for possible publication. The editor will almost always include a clear statement indicating that revision and resubmission is in no way a guarantee of publication. Editors may instruct authors who choose to revise and resubmit their work to also provide a supplemental document, along with the revised manuscript, detailing all the changes they made and explaining their rationale for reviewer-recommended changes that they did not make.

The process of rewriting a manuscript and resubmitting it for another round of peer review is an understandably daunting prospect to authors, particularly since there is no guarantee of publication. Many authors who receive this editorial notice will withdraw their works, modify them or not, and then submit them elsewhere, hoping for a different outcome. Some authors do heed the comments and suggestions provided by editors and reviewers, revise their manuscripts accordingly, and then resubmit to the same journals. Editors who receive resubmitted manuscripts have differing philosophies about assigning reviewers; some believe that a completely fresh and new set of reviewers is best to preserve the integrity of the blind-review process, and others feel that it is useful to include one or more of the original reviewers in order to evaluate the changes that are made or not made. Although the latter option does not constitute a breach in blind review per se, one might argue that manuscript reviewers can have biased perspectives on works they have seen in previous stages. Information relative to these editorial practices may or may not be found in a journal's documentation or openly shared with contributing authors. However, authors are well within their rights to query editors for clarification.

EXAMPLE: Notice to Resubmit Manuscript for Review

Dear [Author(s)]...

Evaluations are completed and returned for your manuscript, "[Manuscript title]." Based on reviewers' comments and suggestions, we are recommending that the manuscript be revised and resubmitted for review. As you will see in the attached comments, the reviewers liked the premise of your study, and also some of the conclusions. Each reviewer, however, identified some necessary changes, and some of those changes are of significant nature. In particular, the reviewers found that [manuscript weaknesses]. The changes that are necessary to address these concerns will substantially modify the overall argument and presentation of your manuscript—thus, the need for a new round of peer review.

We ask that you please read and consider the reviewers' comments, with particular attention to those provided by reviewers 1 and 2, and then let us know what you decide to do with the manuscript. Please note that this editorial decision is not a rejection; instead, it is an indication that the reviewers believe your manuscript can be redeveloped into an article that will contribute to the literature in a unique and effective way. Please note also that resubmission is not a guarantee of publication; substantially revised and rewritten manuscripts must undergo the same professional process of critical evaluation as those that are newly submitted.

We look forward to learning your decision concerning this manuscript. If you have any questions or concerns, please feel free to contact us. We are grateful that you entrusted the results of your scholarly work to [Journal name].

Sincerely,

[Editors]
[Address and contact information]

Reject Manuscript. The manuscript rejection notice is an unpleasant one for authors to receive; it is also a sensitive matter for editors who must issue such a message. The rejection notice informs authors that their work is deemed by a team of peer evaluators and a journal editor to be deficient to a point beyond the help of even significant revisions. Although editors will rarely include such blunt statements, they are essentially reporting that the manuscript is rejected, and that they do not desire to receive or review a revised version. Editors will almost always use more tactfully crafted language, indicating that their decision is based on the reviewers' evaluations. It is important to note, however, that tactfully crafted language can be confusing to authors, particularly to those who are non-native English speakers. In their effort to be polite, editors are sometimes not clear enough about their decision to reject a manuscript outright. As a general rule, unless there is specific language about revising or resubmitting the manuscript, it is rejected.

The deficiencies found in rejected manuscripts are usually manifold, and as noted, they are commonly detailed in the reviewers' comments. Editors may or may not routinely include those comments with a rejection notice, but it is a much more common practice for LIS editors to provide them. Editors will sometimes shy away from providing manuscript evaluations if they contain harshly worded criticisms. In such instances editors will often moderate the criticisms, and then provide a revised version of them to authors as a professional courtesy. If an editor's decision to reject is in contrast to the reviewers' comments, it is likely that the editor simply removed harsher criticisms. It is also important to note that reviewers are commonly asked to provide separate reports for authors and editors. Reviewers may be inclined to write gentler evaluations for authors, and to provide more bluntly worded evaluations for editors.

Receiving a rejection notice is understandably disappointing, but authors are reminded that it is a very common experience for all scholars, and that the experience can ultimately lead to a more positive outcome. To begin, an editor will not send a manuscript for review unless he or she recognizes some potential for publication; that is the first hurdle. Next, the reviewers' evaluations and any supplemental input from editors can and should be used to improve a manuscript. Some of the evaluations may be unpleasant, but reviewers do not provide comments or suggestions with the intent to offend; their role is to provide informed and substantive feedback relative to a prospective contribution to the professional literature. It is their responsibility to identify what they perceive to be particular strengths or weaknesses in manuscripts that are assigned to them. Finally, it is altogether possible that a manuscript will be received differently by the editor and reviewers of another journal. As detailed in the Elements of Selecting the Right Journal chapter, publishing a scholarly paper is largely dependent upon matching the manuscript to the right publication. It is a very common occurrence for rejected manuscripts to ultimately be accepted elsewhere, and sometimes with only modest revisions.

EXAMPLE: Notice of Manuscript Rejection

Dear [Authors(s)]...

Thank you for submitting your manuscript, "[Manuscript tile]," for review to [Journal name]. [Number] reviewers, all experts in your field, have provided evaluations of your manuscript; the editors also read and considered your work. Based on the reviewers' comments and suggestions, and also on our own reading, we have reached an editorial decision. We regret to say that although the topic of the manuscript is [editors' input], and that the reviewers appreciated [reviewers' input], the expressed concerns about the overall work preclude its publication in [Journal name]. As you will see in the attached evaluations, the reviewers' concerns are consistent across all of their evaluations. In particular, the reviewers noted [manuscript weaknesses].

We understand that it is difficult to receive a negative decision for a manuscript submission, but we hope that you will find the reviews helpful in moving forward with this work. We also hope that you will continue to consider [Journal name] as an outlet for your scholarly works. Thank you again for allowing us the privilege of reviewing your manuscript.

Best regards,

[Editor]
[Address and contact information]

Responding to Editorial Decisions

Information presented in this section pertains to authors who receive any of the following non-acceptance editorial decisions regarding their submitted works: revisions required, resubmit for review, or rejected. Any discussion relative to acceptance notifications is unwarranted here; recipients of these satisfying decisions need only to follow editorial instructions and then to celebrate the well-deserved good news.

Editorial decisions of non-acceptance are an inevitable reality for all scholars. An investigation by Campanario (1996) showed that it is even common for authors who win the Nobel Prize to first have their prize-winning works rejected by journal editors. Manuscript decisions of non-acceptance should be regarded by authors as nothing more than a natural part of the publishing process. It is not an exaggeration, however, to state that the manner in which authors respond these decisions is as much of an indicator of their scholarly ability as the quality of their actual work. As Belcher (2009) asserts:

> How you respond to journal decisions about your submitted articles will determine your academic career. That may seem to be strong language, but it is true. If you take negative journal decisions as accurate assessments of your aptitude for scholarship, if you fail to revise when advised to do so, or if you abandon an article just because it was rejected, you will not do well in your chosen profession. Those who persevere despite abuse, dismissal, and rejection are those who succeed. (p.287)

Responding to the Revisions Required Notice. As detailed earlier in this chapter, the editorial decision that a manuscript requires revisions is generally a positive indicator (see Revisions Required section). Virtually all manuscripts require some form of adjustment or change; that, too, is a natural part of the publication process. Authors receiving this notice should heed the recommended changes, meticulously revise their work (see Manuscript Revisions section), and then return it to their corresponding journal editor as quickly as possible. Alacrity is strategically important here; authors should resubmit their work while it is still fresh in the mind of the journal editor. The editor will reread the manuscript, with particular attention to the areas where he or she and the reviewers recommended specific changes. At this stage of the process, it is highly unlikely that the reviewers will be called upon to reread the manuscript. With the revised manuscript in hand, it is the editor's responsibility to judge whether or not the suggested changes were adequately addressed, and then to issue a decision.

Responding to the Resubmit for Review Notice. The main decision facing authors who receive the resubmit for review notice is whether or not to continue working toward publication in the same journal. There are no authoritative statistics to show how LIS authors generally decide in this circumstance, but there are always indicators to help them with their decision. The overall tone of the editor's decision message and the content of the reviewers' evaluations are the two most important considerations. If an editor makes a point of encouraging an author to move forward with his or her work, and if the reviewers' comments are similarly promising in nature, then the submitting author may wish to continue working toward publication in the same journal. Authors are reminded, however, that resubmission to the same journal is never a guarantee of publication. If an editor's decision message does not align with reviewers' comments, there is a reason for that, and authors should consider submitting their work elsewhere. Authors are furthermore reminded that it is commonplace for bounced manuscripts to ultimately be accepted elsewhere, and sometimes with only modest revisions.

As noted in the Resubmit for Review section, manuscripts resubmitted to the same journal may or may not be evaluated by one or more of the original reviewers. Authors who are deciding whether or not to resubmit are well within their rights to query editors for clarification on this matter. Authors are also encouraged to review the Elements of Selecting the Right Journal chapter to guide their decision on whether or not to resubmit to the same publication. In particular, authors are discouraged from continuing their work with any given journal merely because of its relative prestige in the discipline. Matching one's work with the right journal will naturally generate interest among an appropriate, like-minded readership, which is, or should be the primary goal of publishing a scholarly paper.

Responding to the Rejection Notice. Authors who receive the editorial decision that their manuscript has been rejected are generally faced with four options: They may submit their unrevised work elsewhere, revise their work and submit elsewhere, challenge the editorial decision, or abandon their work altogether. The rejection notice usually includes reviewer evaluations, and sometimes the editor will also, in good faith, provide the names of other journals that may be appropriate for the rejected work. If the reason given for rejection is that the manuscript is not a good fit for the journal, and if no significant revisions are suggested, then the author may find success submitting their work elsewhere with only modest changes. However, most manuscripts that are deemed to be a poor fit for a journal are rejected prior to review. It is more common for rejected manuscripts to include substantial criticisms and recommended revisions. Although these criticisms and recommendations will be difficult to read, authors are encouraged to regard them as a form of professional mentoring. Given that the reviewers and editors have done their job well, the rejection notice will almost always include helpful and instructive information. Authors are also reminded that reviewer evaluations and editorial decisions are not gospel; rejected manuscripts are often received differently when submitted elsewhere.

Authors are within their rights to challenge an editorial decision. Although this is a more common occurrence with journals in scientific, technical, engineering, and medical disciplines, it is not unprecedented in LIS. Authors may believe that reviewer evaluations are biased, flawed, or even unfair, but they should bear in mind that editors understand very well the imperfections of peer review. Those imperfections are almost always considered during the complex process of making and issuing an editorial decision. Authors may appeal or even protest reviewer evaluations, but they are cautioned to avoid emotional retorts. Most LIS editors have received responses of displeasure; they are more likely to be moved by reasoned arguments than by rants or retaliatory remarks. More to the point, there is little evidence to suggest that challenges to editorial decisions are worth pursuing in LIS or in any of the social sciences. Simon, Bakanic, and McPhail (1986) conducted a study of author challenges to editorial decisions issued for a premier sociology journal; the results of their research showed that only 13 percent of challenges resulted in overturned editorial decisions (p. 259). It should also be noted that very few LIS journals have formal appeal processes. Authors of rejected manuscripts are likely to find greater success by focusing their time and energy on resubmitting their work to another journal.

Authors of rejected manuscripts may also face the decision of whether or not to abandon their work altogether. Research in this area shows an evolution of how authors decide when faced with this decision. The likelihood that authors will resubmit elsewhere is greater today than in the past; this is likely a result of the expanded professional literature. However, there is also evidence showing that an unexpectedly high percentage of authors continue to abandon their work. In their pivotal investigation, Garvey, Lin, and Tomita (1972) discovered that nearly one-third of scholars in the physical and social sciences abandoned not only their rejected manuscripts, but they also "abandoned the subject-matter area of their article" (p. 214). Later, Rotton, et al. (1995) showed that 83 percent of the social science scholars included in their study resubmitted rejected manuscripts to other journals, but that 74 percent of the study participants had abandoned their work at least once as a result of rejection. There is limited research in this area that is specific to LIS, but Hernon, Smith, and Croxen (1993) did showed that 40 percent of the manuscripts rejected by *College & Research Libraries* were ultimately published elsewhere. The general rule for authors is that they should only consider abandoning their work if it has been rejected a minimum of three times, if the reasons given for rejection are consistent from each journal, and if those given reasons are unresolvable. Otherwise, authors are encouraged to be confident in their work, and to be persistent in finding the right journal for it.

5.5 Manuscript Revisions

Much of what goes into effectively revising one's manuscript is already detailed in the Elements of Writing Well chapter and in the Manuscript Preparation section of this text. There are, however, some unique elements of the revision process for scholarly papers, and there are some important reminders. Authors are encouraged to consult the following checklist of best practices for revising the scholarly paper manuscript:

- *Revise immediately.* Do not allow a demanding schedule to interfere with the publishing process; the incomplete manuscript must be prioritized. Besides, authors commonly find that revising their work is a less time consuming task than they had expected. Authors should commence with revisions while their work and their consulted source materials are fresh in mind; this will accelerate the revision process. As noted, it is also an important strategy to return one's revised work while it is still familiar to the journal editor, and before another author submits a paper on the same subject matter.

- *Organize revisions.* It can be challenging to synthesize and keep track of all of the recommended changes that come with reviewer evaluations and editorial decisions. Editors will sometimes provide guidance in terms of what suggested changes they believe require the most or least attention. Still, authors should treat all of the reviewer suggestions seriously, and the best way to do so is to collate them in a practicable manner. This may involve fashioning a spreadsheet, creating a mark-up version of one's manuscript (e.g., the Track Changes function in Microsoft Word), or even printing copies to mark-up by hand. Authors will have their own preferences for organizing revisions; the key is that they do so in an efficient and thorough manner.

- *Clarify revisions.* The revisions that are recommended by reviewers and editors may be unclear, and sometimes they may even be contradictory. Authors should not be shy about contacting editors for clarification; it is an editor's responsibility to provide the necessary guidance. Importantly, however, authors may not concur with all of the suggested changes. It is in their best interest to only inquire about those recommendations that they intend to address; otherwise, authors may be instructed to make revisions with which they disagree.

- *Enumerate revisions.* Editors will commonly request of authors who are revising and returning manuscripts to also include a separate document with concise descriptions of the changes made and explanations for the changes not made. Even when editors do not ask, it is a good practice for authors to include this document. Although authors may not make each of the recommended changes to a manuscript, it is vital that they address all of them. Enumerating one's revisions serves many purposes. To begin, it helps authors to keep track of any and all manuscript adjustments; it helps editors to quickly identify changes that have made and the quality of them; and it demonstrates authors' willingness to participate professionally in the publication process. Finally, listing and explaining the recommended changes that are not made provides an opportunity for authors to address elements of a manuscript that they believe the reviewers may have misread or misinterpreted.

- *Avoid over-correction.* It is a common experience for authors to over-react to reviewers' suggested changes. Those suggestions commonly require just minor additions or adjustments: an added sentence for clarification, a qualifying term, or a cited reference to bridge previous works to one's own. Authors should take particular care to avoid making unnecessary changes or those that are not recommended by reviewers or editors.

- *Revise length of manuscript.* The editorial decision will often include a recommendation to either lengthen or shorten the submitted manuscript; the latter of these recommendations is far more common. There is a general tendency for reviewers to suggest expanded works, or specific elements of them, and for editors to suggest shorter ones. If reviewer and editor recommendations for length are at odds, then authors should seek clarification and direction from the editor. Authors can use these contradictory recommendations as an advantage for negotiating which changes the editor sees as vital, and which ones may be regarded as less important or unnecessary. Authors should also consult with the editor when manuscript expansion is recommended beyond a journal's guidelines for word or page limits. Strategies for shortening an LIS manuscript are standard; the typical scholarly paper will include elements that can be cropped or even stricken without having an impact on the overall argument or presentation. Authors looking to shorten their works should begin by removing unnecessary appendices, background information, block quotations, descriptions of previous works, figures, and footnotes.

- *Revise grammar, style, and quality of writing.* Reviewers and editors will always comment accordingly when the quality of writing in manuscripts is substandard. In some instances mark-up versions of authors' works are provided with directions for specific changes that are needed, but it is more common for reviewers and editors to simply insist that the quality of writing must be improved. Authors who receive these comments are encouraged to comb through the Elements of Writing Well chapter and Manuscript Preparation section of this text for ways in which to improve their writing. More importantly, authors are strenuously encouraged to ask colleagues who are skilled editors and writers to read their work and to provide honest feedback. Authors may also consider hiring a professional copyeditor. This may seem to be an expensive proposition, but authors should consider the greater costs of not publishing their work in terms of wasted time and energy, and the possible implications in terms of professional appointment, renewal, promotion, and tenure.

Revising Specific Elements of Manuscript

The editorial decision will almost always include a recommendation to revise specific parts of the scholarly paper. Authors who receive such recommendations are strongly encouraged to consult the Elements of the Scholarly Paper section of this text. The most commonly concerning parts of the typical LIS manuscript are the introduction, the literature review, the discussion, and the conclusion.

- **Revise introduction.** In terms of the introduction, reviewers will often comment that definitions are unclear, or that arguments or assertions are not supported in subsequent sections of the paper. Such comments may be the result of poor reviewing, but they should be addressed nonetheless. Definitions can typically be improved or clarified by the simple addition of a few words or a qualifying sentence, and introductory arguments or assertions can usually be reinforced by adding evidentiary aspects that are already included in the literature review, discussion, or conclusion sections of a paper.
- **Revise literature review.** The most common critiques of the literature review are as follows: it is unnecessarily long; it includes coverage of irrelevant works; it is missing critical works; or it does not suffi-

ciently establish the need for what the authors are arguing or presenting. If authors disagree with any of these reviewer comments, then they should include an explanation in the supplemental revisions document that they provide to the editor. Shortening the literature review is ordinarily an easy task; authors can typically start by removing or minimizing lengthy block or in-text quotations. Authors can also crop lengthy descriptions of other scholars' works, or they can simply delete irrelevant or unnecessary ones. When reviewers recommend the coverage or inclusion of additional source materials, they will often cite them specifically or point to an area of the literature that is necessary for authors to effectively argue the need for their own work. Although reading and synthesizing those works will improve authors' scholarly capacity, it is often unnecessary. Simply citing the additional works and framing them in the context of the main topic will generally suffice. More intensive and time consuming changes are necessary when reviewers or editors assert that the literature review does not adequately establish the need for what authors are arguing or presenting; in these instances, authors are highly encouraged to review the Elements of the Scholarly Paper section of this text for improvement strategies.

- *Revise discussion and conclusion.* Although this deviates from the standard social science paper, the LIS manuscript frequently includes elements of the discussion and the conclusion in one combined section. Reviewers or editors will commonly report that authors have failed to effectively use this section to interpret results, draw conclusions, assert implications, or provide a clear summary of the manuscript's argument and significance. It is true that some manuscripts are poorly argued or lack the necessary evidence to support authors' conclusions, but it is more common that the discussion and conclusion section can be bolstered by simply reiterating essential points that are presented in other sections the manuscript. Finally, the typical LIS paper is 20-25 pages long in manuscript form; with that in mind, reviewers and editors sometimes need to have all of a paper's essential points provided in a cumulative summation in order to fully understand the significance of what is being argued or presented.

Chapter 5 Appendix

Reviewer Guidelines for Communications in Information Literacy (CIL)

Introduction

The purpose of this document is to provide CIL reviewers with a toolkit for reviewing manuscripts, and generally, to guide them through the review process.

Reviewer Guidelines

1. Writing the Report
2. Reviewing the Content
3. Determining Quality & Significance

1. Writing the Report

Role of the Reviewer

The peer reviewer has two basic roles: to determine if the article is suitable for publication in CIL, and to help the authors to improve their manuscript in order to make it "publication ready". The reviewer will examine the paper in terms of its overall value, the quality of the research and the way it is presented, and the effectiveness of the final product. The amount of time necessary to do an effective peer review varies greatly, and is dependent on the subject matter, length, and quality of the manuscript, as well as the reviewer's own familiarity with the topic (although the reviewer should always have some expertise in that area).

Benos, Kirk, and Hall (2003), in their article *How to Review a Paper,* give a thorough discussion of the role of the reviewer, outlining several key obligations. These include:

- Upholding confidentiality. The reviewer should respect the privacy of the author by keeping the manuscript and its contents confidential. The submission should not be shared or discussed in detail with any third party (49).
- Maintaining objectivity. The reviewer should inform the editor of any potential conflicts of interest before commencing the review. For example, if the reviewer is able identify the author, it may not, ultimately, affect the integrity of the review, but should be disclosed. The reviewer should decline any review if s/he feels his/her objectivity will be compromised (50).
- Having significant knowledge. The manuscript should fall within the reviewer's area of expertise. If the reviewer believes that s/he lacks the expertise to make a thorough evaluation of the manuscript, s/he should decline the review, explaining the reason (50).

Content & Structure

The peer review should be readable and as succinct as possible while guiding the authors toward an effective revision. The reviewer should keep in mind that s/he is providing information to guide both the author and the journal editors; although it is not necessary to submit separate reviews, the reviewer can submit additional comments to the editor in addition to those that will be seen by the author in the final review.

To aid the reviewer in developing a well-organized and succinct review, s/he should have an overall sense of the manuscript before attempting a detailed critique. It may be helpful to begin the process by "pre-reading" the article—reviewing the introduction, conclusion, and major headings—followed by an initial reading of the manuscript, from beginning to end, without pen in hand.

There is no "one way" to organize a review—the reviewer's approach will depend largely on the concerns and recommendations associated with that particular manuscript. However, Seals and Tanaka (2000) suggest organizing comments into minor, "housekeeping" concerns and major concerns "on which the acceptability of the manuscript depends" (p. 57). This approach can help the reviewer to decide what should be included in the review and what should be omitted: if a comment does not have a significant impact on whether the article should be accepted, it may be a minor criticism, and the reviewer may ultimately choose to omit from the review entirely.

Tone & Balance

Above all, the reviewer has a responsibility to treat the author being reviewed with respect. A little kindness goes a long way—even if the manuscript is very problematic the reviewer should try to identify strengths and provide some positive feedback, to motivate and encourage the author and to balance criticism. The value of even the most thorough review will be lost if it is couched in terms that are sarcastic or unhelpfully critical. As Provenzale and Stanley note in their article, *A Systematic Guide to Reviewing a Manuscript* (2006), "the overriding theme is that reviewers should treat the manuscripts they review as they would like their own to be treated".

The reviewer should not, however, worry unnecessarily if more of the review is devoted to providing constructive criticism than positive feedback; even with very strong manuscripts this is often the case. As Seals and Tanaka (2000) observe, "The reviewer should comment on both the strengths and the weaknesses of the paper, although the latter usually requires more space, because the referee needs to explain his or her concerns and how those concerns can be resolved" (p. 57). This is not, in itself, the mark of an unbalanced review, but rather one that adequately and fairly informs the reader.

Dos & Don'ts

Further to the above recommendations, there are a number of essential "Dos and Don'ts" that the reviewer should always keep in mind when preparing a review. These fundamentals are listed in the table below:

DON'T	DO
...make vague, general comments about the quality of the manuscript.	...be specific, by giving examples and suggesting solutions.

DON'T	DO
...take on the role of copy editor. Grammar, spelling, typing edits are outside the scope of the peer review.	...if necessary, mention large-scale problems in these areas, giving just a few examples to show where the problem occurs.
...make disrespectful comments of the "so what?" variety.	...treat the authors you are reviewing with kindness and respect.
...argue with the author. Instead, ask for clarification or suggest ways to strengthening the author's position (Maner 2001b).	...focus on how effectively the author supports his/her argument, rather than your own opinion (Maner 2001b).

Final Recommendations

The final task of the peer reviewer is to make a recommendation regarding the manuscript. CIL provides four choices from which the reviewer must choose: Accept Submission; Revisions Required; Resubmit for Review; and Decline Submission.

- Accept Submission: The overall quality and significance of the manuscript is appropriate for publication in CIL. (Note: Even the very best of manuscripts will require at least some minor revisions.)
- Revisions Required: Revisions are required in order for the manuscript to be appropriate for publication in CIL. The manuscript "should" be accepted for publication, assuming that necessary revisions are made. (Note: Please specify the necessary revisions.)
- Resubmit for Review: The manuscript requires changes of a significant enough nature that a revised version will need to undergo the

full review process. Authors may resubmit the revised manuscript for review, though there is no guarantee of acceptance.

- Decline Submission: Even with significant revisions, the overall quality and significance of the manuscript is inappropriate for publication in CIL.

In some cases, the recommendation will be obvious after an initial reading of the manuscript, but if the reviewer is unsure, the best strategy is to develop the written review before deciding on the final recommendation; as Seals and Tanaka (2000) note, the reviewer will often "have a clearer position…after undergoing the intellectual process" (p. 58). The reviewer's final recommendation will be based on a number of considerations, including the uniqueness of the article and interest to the profession; appropriateness for publication in CIL; quality of presentation; and validity of the research.

2. Reviewing the Content

The Title

The title provides a first impression regarding the content of an article, and will often have a significant impact on whether or not a reader chooses to look further. The reviewer should consider the following when evaluating the proposed title:

- Does the title "make sense", and will it give the reader a general idea of what the article is about?
- Does it accurately reflect the content of the article?
- Is there anything about the title that might mislead the reader?
- Should the title be revised in some way to provide further information? For example, should a key concept, theme, or methodology be mentioned?

The Introduction

The introduction lays the foundation for the rest of the paper; if the article is not adequately introduced, the significance and usefulness of its content may be lost on the reader. Likewise, if the introduction does not accurately reflect the content of the article, the reader may feel confused or misled. Consider the following questions when reviewing the introduction:

- Does the introduction include a clear, complete and concise statement of the authors' purpose, thesis or hypothesis?
- Is there an overview of the goals, methods and organization of the article (Maner, 2001a)?
- Are the unique or significant aspects of the paper described? Do the authors explain how their findings "extend previous knowledge in a meaningful way" (Seals & Tanaka, 2000, p. 56)?
- Is the introduction appropriately succinct? Is there information which should be omitted or moved to another section of the paper?
- Return to the introduction once the whole paper has been read—does the body of the paper reflect the purpose, thesis and goals set out in the introduction?

Images & Illustrations

Images and illustrations should be included—and only included—to enhance the reader's understanding of the article. Consider the following when reviewing illustrations:

- Does the image have a direct bearing on the reader's understanding of the article? Does it clarify or illustrate a complicated fact or concept?
- Does the image accurately serve its function as described in the text of the article?
- Have any illustrations been included which are either decorative, or too simplistic to usefully enhance the reader's understanding of the text?
- Are there places where an illustration would be useful in order to enhance the reader's understanding of the text? If so, what kind of illustration should the author include?
- Are all illustrations properly labelled, both in the text of the article and on the image itself, so that the reader can make the appropriate connections between text and image?

Figures & Tables

As with images and illustrations, figures and tables should only be included to enhance the reader's understanding of the article. Consider the following when reviewing figures and tables:

- Does the figure or table have a direct bearing on the reader's understanding of the article? Does it necessary to demonstrate what is presented in the text of the article?
- Does the figure or table accurately serve its function as described in the text of the article?
- Have any figures or tables been included that are unnecessary, too simplistic, or too large to usefully enhance the reader's understanding of the text?
- Are there places where a figure or table would be useful in order to enhance the reader's understanding of the text?
- Are all figures and tables properly labelled, both in the text of the article and on the figures and tables themselves, so that the reader can make the appropriate connections between them and the text?

Use of Sources

The reviewer should decide whether sources are used appropriately in the article. Where necessary, the reviewer should locate and examine cited sources to ensure they have been accurately represented. Although the reviewer might make note of any large-scale citation problems, detailed editing of the citations themselves should be left to the copy editor. Instead, the reviewer should focus on the following questions:

- Is the content appropriately supported using references to other sources?
- Have the cited sources been accurately and fairly represented?
- Are there any statements or arguments that should be substantiated using secondary sources?
- Is the overall quality of the citations themselves acceptable? For example, are there mistakes or stylistic inconsistencies?

Style & Organization

The reviewer should pay attention to the overall style and organization of the paper, in order to decide if it is logical and appropriate to the journal.

Although the peer reviewer should not engage in detailed copy editing, large-scale stylistic problems should be noted. Consider the following questions when reviewing a manuscript for style and organization:

- Does the manuscript follow the basic directions set out in the Author Guidelines for CIL?
- Is the paper clearly written, logically organized, and easy to understand?
- Is the reviewer able to follow the "overall logical structure" throughout the article? If not, at what point does the organization or the argument deteriorate (Cornell 2007)?
- Is the paper clearly divided into logical sections? Are there sections that should be further subdivided, or should some content be relocated to other sections of the paper?
- Is the article appropriately concise? Is there repetitive or extraneous content that should be edited or removed? If so, which sections are they (be specific)?
- Are there gaps in the paper? Have useful or important sections been omitted, or does anything need to be discussed or developed more fully?

3. Determining Quality & Significance
Significance of the Article

The reviewer should consider the article in terms of its significance to readers, as well as it's appropriateness for publication in CIL. To help make these judgements, the reviewer may need to do a scan of the literature available on the topic, and review the scope and focus of CIL. When making these judgements, it is also useful to ask:

- Does the paper present a unique or novel perspective? Does it introduce new ideas, or offer a new perspective on existing ideas (Seals & Tanaka, 2000, p. 58; Association for Preservation, 2009)?
- Is the subject of the article significant or important to the field? Do you believe that CIL readers will be interested in what it has to offer?
- Does the paper fit within the stated focus, scope, and guidelines of the journal? Does it seem like an appropriate addition to CIL?

Quality of Research

Where original research is presented, the reviewer should consider the quality of both the presentation and the methodological approach. The following questions will help with this analysis:

- Have the researchers employed suitable methods (e.g. were subjects selected appropriately, and have they employed valid survey, observation, or experimentation strategies)?
- Has a rationale been provided for the chosen methodology, and is it reasonable? Are there alternative approaches the author's might have adopted, and if so, do they explain their choice (Provenzale & Stanley, 2006, p. 94)?
- Do the authors present any unnecessary or unexplained data? If so, should it be explained, or omitted from the article?
- Have the authors provided enough information for you to evaluate the accuracy of their conclusions? Are there any gaps in the author's research (primary or secondary) that should be addressed? If so, what additions are needed?
- Are the author's findings believable? If they are not, what do you find questionable or contradictory?
- Do the authors accurately and logically interpret their own research findings? Can you think of other interpretations besides the ones that have been presented?
- Have the authors presented and discussed limitations of the study "in a good faith manner that properly informs the reader" (Seals & Tanaka, 2000, p. 55)?

Evidence of Bias

Closely connected to quality of research is the need for unbiased presentation of the authors' findings. The reviewer should consider the following questions when examining the paper for signs of bias:

- Are the arguments and findings presented in a way that seems objective, even-handed, and fair?
- Do the authors' present opinions as though they were factual information (Maner, 2001a)?

- Does the author appear to make assumptions or jump to conclusions, based on incomplete or inadequate evidence (Maner, 2001a)?

Reference List

Association for Preservation Technology International (2009). *APT Bulletin: The Journal of Preservation Technology. Guidelines for peer reviewers.* Retrieved from: http://www.apti.org/publications/peer-guidelines.cfm.

Benos, D.J., Kirk, K.L., & Hall, J.E. (2003). How to Review a Paper. *Advances in Physiology Education, 27,* 47-52. doi:10.1152/advan.00057.2002.

Cornell University (2007). *Peer Review Guidelines.* Retrieved From http://instruct1.cit.cornell.edu/courses/taresources/PR2.PDF.

Maner, M. (2001a). *The Research Process: Revision Questions for Peer Collaborators.* Retrieved from http://www.mhhe.com/mayfieldpub/maner/resources/peer3.htm.

Maner, M. (2001b). *The Research Process: Some "Do's" and "Don'ts" of Peer Evaluation.* Retrieved from http://www.mhhe.com/mayfieldpub/maner/resources/peer5.htm.

Provenzale, J.M., & Stanley, R.J. (2006). A Systematic Guide to Reviewing a Manuscript [Electronic version]. *Journal of Nuclear Medicine Technology, 34,* 92-99.

Seals, D. R. & Tanaka, H. (2000). Manuscript Peer Review: A Helpful Checklist for Students and Novice Referees [Electronic version]. *Advances in Physiology Education, 23,* 52-58.

Notes

1. December 2009. Janet Goosney, Memorial University of Newfoundland Christopher Hollister, University at Buffalo

6

Elements of the Scholarly Book

There are different ways in which LIS authors involve themselves in the creation of books; they may be authors of individual chapters, authors of entire volumes, or editors of compilations. Authors who are working on book chapters are encouraged to review the Elements of Writing Well and the Elements of the Scholarly Paper chapters of this text. The present chapter is devoted to writing or editing complete volumes, which is a substantially different undertaking. Particular emphasis is given to the writing of scholarly books, although much of the discussion can be applied to textbooks as well.

It typically takes one to two years for the scholarly book to run its metamorphic course from a proposal to an actual publication. Some scholars are able to develop their works faster, and some are slower, and some publishers are more efficient than others in terms of production. As a general rule, however, authors should plan for a period of one to two years; this amount of time, alone, makes the development of a scholarly book far different than that of an academic paper. Although there are numerous overlapping considerations in both forms of writing, publishing the scholarly book also involves processes that are different from those of scholarly papers: to wit, selecting a publisher, writing a proposal, and developing and adhering to a rigorous writing plan. Each of these processes is fully delineated in the present chapter.

First and foremost, the decision to write or edit a book should be driven solely by the nature of the main topic. Also, the subject matter or the author's approach to subject matter should be fresh, new, and worthy as an addition to the professional literature. As Crawford (2003) contends, "You should write books for the same primary reason you write articles: because you have something to say" (p. 82). However, the subject matter should also lend itself to being presented in a book, whether print or electronic. That is, the form of the book-length text should be guided by the function of effectively communicating its main subject matter.

The possibilities of scholarly books are generally more open than those of scholarly papers. Books are less confining in terms of prescribed format, length, style, and tone. Scholarly books are also broader in scope than scholarly papers, and they entail a greater depth of subject coverage. As a result, books ordinarily require a more significant commitment in terms of time and effort. Still, the fundamental elements of effective academic writing, as they are discussed throughout this text, apply to scholarly books just as they do to scholarly papers.

The unfortunate reality for many scholarly books in the social sciences is that they are not always written purely for the purpose of expressing new ideas. As Swain (2012) bluntly asserted, "Academics don't write to be read; they write to be published" (para. 1). In that same vein, there is a significant percentage of academics who do not read scholarly books for the purpose of learning new ideas, but rather to glean information in support of their own research and writing projects. Happily, the discipline of LIS is more functional in nature than most other social sciences, and as a result, the professional literature is more focused on the sharing and learning of new ideas, and it is less focused on uninspired publishing motivations.

6.1 *Library and Information Science Book Publishers*

The publishing marketplace for scholarly LIS books is considerably different than it is for scholarly LIS papers; most notably, there are far fewer options for authors to consider. In Crawford's (2003) excellent guidebook, he lists the small number of publishers that regularly offer new LIS titles; those are led by the American Library Association (ALA) and select divisions, Greenwood, Libraries Unlimited, Neal-Schuman, and a few others. There is also a small number of complementary publishers that irregularly offer new LIS titles. However, recent developments in the LIS book marketplace have narrowed the field of potential publishers even further: ABC-Clio acquired Greenwood, Libraries Unlimited acquired Linworth Publishing, and the ALA acquired Neal-Schuman. Although the imprints remain for these acquired publishers, the overall number of relevant publishing houses for LIS authors continues to shrink. Still, prospective authors should not be discouraged by this; there will always be eager publishers awaiting new ideas that are coupled with effective writing.

Publishing scholarly LIS books is also different from that of scholarly LIS papers in another important way: There are no academic publishers that regularly offer new LIS titles. The marketplace is primarily dominated by one professional association—the ALA and its divisions—and a small number of commercial publishers. Increasingly, however, LIS professionals are exploring unconventional publishing models: namely, open access and self-publishing. The open access model is driven by the possibilities of the free web, and self-publishing model is made more viable by way of web-based services such as print-on-demand. The open access model may be attractive to authors for a variety of reasons, including increased visibility for their work, increased measures of impact and prestige, new directions for scholarly communication, and even professional LIS values and philosophies that run counter to the practices of commercial publishers. To date, the most active LIS publisher of open access books is the ALA and its divisions. The self-publishing model may also be attractive to authors for a variety of reasons, including the failure to publish with a conventional publisher, or the desire to control more aspects of the publication process, including production and royalties. Authors who are considering the self-publishing model are cautioned to remember the invaluable role of the editor in the publishing process; without a professional editor's input, the quality of any author's writing is likely to suffer.

Selecting Book Publishers

Although the number of choices is somewhat limited, selecting the right publisher for one's book is paramount. To reiterate some essential starting points, the decision to write a book should be driven by an idea, that idea should be new, relevant, and timely to the discipline and the profession, and it should be appropriate for a book-length work. If these criteria are effectively articulated in a book proposal, and if that proposal is submitted to an appropriate publisher for that subject matter, then the publisher is likely to accept it. Authors are cautioned to dismiss any lofty considerations of wealth or prestige. Regardless of the publisher, authors will not generate great wealth by way of LIS book sales, nor will they be considered for Pulitzer or Nobel Prizes by virtue of their scholarly works. Relative sales and prestige are driven solely by the newness, effectiveness, and usefulness of ideas that are presented to a targeted readership within the discipline.

The publishers of LIS texts have established and proven infrastructures for marketing their products to targeted audiences. Still, the ALA and its divisions have some key advantages. To begin, authors who choose to publish with ALA are supporting their own professional association. Books published by ALA divisions, in particular, are highly regarded by their constituencies, and they are ordinarily considered to be prestigious contributions to the literature. This is an important concern for academic librarians who need to demonstrate the overall impact of their work for promotion or tenure. Additionally, publishing with the ALA and its divisions commonly leads to complementary, organization-sponsored opportunities relative to the subject matter of one's book. Such opportunities may include invitations to give conference presentations, teach online courses, lead web-based seminars, or participate in other professional development or continuing education-related activities.

As a general rule, commercial publishers of LIS texts have the ability to offer authors better-paying contracts, but when compared to ALA contracts, the differences are minimal. Commercial publishers usually have more money to devote to production quality, as well. Still, LIS professionals should know that better royalties and higher production costs will ultimately result in more expensive texts, and that should resonate deeply for any professionals who have collection development responsibilities. Authors are by no means discouraged from opting to publish their works with commercial agencies; the discipline has strong, long-standing, and highly important relationships with a handful of commercial LIS publishers. Still, authors are reminded that there are many factors to consider, and each one has important implications. Authors are also reminded to review the Elements of Selecting the Right Journal chapter of this text; there are numerous overlapping considerations relative to the criteria that one should use for selecting book and journal publishers.

Querying Book Publishers

Querying book publishers is similar to querying journal editors in many respects, but there are unique elements as well. Although it is not always necessary, it is highly recommended that authors query publishers in advance of submitting their formal proposals. Most LIS publishers accept proposals that arrive without prior author contact; those works are typically valued and treated in the same professional manner as proposals that arrive with prior author contact. However, the query serves three critically important purposes for book authors. To begin, the query helps to initiate a positive and professional author-publisher rapport; this may seem a trivial point to some, but the author-publisher relationship is strategically significant for both parties. Next, the query generates a response that either confirms or rebuts an author's belief that his or her book is appropriate for the selected publisher. Publishers will consider specific elements of the query before they respond: the appropriateness of the subject matter, the timeliness of the subject matter, the estimated length of the completed text, the potential sales in target markets, and any number of other elements that may be of particular concern. For authors, knowing ahead of time that a manuscript may or may not be the right fit for a publisher saves a considerable amount of time and energy that should otherwise be devoted to developing a smart and targeted proposal. Finally, authors can typically benefit by gleaning useful information from publishers' responses in order to improve the chances that their proposals will ultimately be accepted there or elsewhere.

Authors should always make it as easy as possible for publishers to conduct their business. In terms of the query, it should be professional, but above all things, it should be brief and succinct. If publishers are interested, then authors will be asked to provide all the necessary details in a formal book proposal. For ease-of-use and expediency, LIS publishers conduct much of their business through email. Authors are encouraged to contact publishers by way of the email address listed on their web site. The query should be formally addressed, and it should include the following elements:

- Proposed book title and very brief description.
- Brief description of the purpose and unique nature of the proposed book, and also the need for it in the discipline or in the profession.
- Brief assertion of usefulness to the publisher's target audience; reason for selecting the publisher; evidence of familiarity with publisher's catalog.

- Estimated length of completed book.
- Estimated time table for completing the book.
- Evidence of expertise in the subject matter and/or evidence of relevant experience.
- Evidence of scholarly ability; attached résumé or curriculum vitae.
- Awards, grants, or other activities associated with the book.

EXAMPLE: Book Publisher Query [Email]

Dear [Dr., Mr., Ms.] [First name, Last name]:

Good day to you. The purpose of this message is to determine your interest in an idea that I have for submitting a book proposal to [Publisher name]. The working title for my proposed book is [Book title], and as the title suggests, it will be [concise description of approach and subject matter]. The focus of my work will be [unique, distinguishing features]. To date, there are no books published about [subject matter] that include such an approach.

As the [Position title] Librarian for [Institution name], I am required to [relevant experience], and as you know, librarians across the profession are faced with the same challenges. This has been the focus of my research for five years. If you will kindly refer to my attached résumé, you will find that I have already published two refereed journal articles and one book chapter that are based on [relevant subject matter], and with this book I intend to [unique selling point].

In terms of practicalities, I have already begun my work on this project and intend to have it completed by [date]. I estimate that the length of the completed work will be 250 double-spaced pages in manuscript form and 200 pages in typeset form. I chose to query [Publisher name]

EXAMPLE: Book Publisher Query [Email], cont.

because it is a publisher that specializes in books devoted to [subject matter], and also because my proposed book is intended for a broad audience of [targeted readership].

Would please be kind enough to indicate whether or not [Publisher name] is interested in my idea for this book? If so, I will promptly complete and submit the official proposal form on your web site. Thank you very much for your time and consideration. I look forward to hearing from you.

Sincerely,

[Name]
[Affiliation]
[Address and contact information]

6.2 *The Book Proposal*

For numerous reasons, the proposal is the key to publishing a book. Obviously, a proposal is an author's selling pitch to a publisher, and for that reason alone it needs to be an exceptionally well-considered and well-crafted document. Beyond that, however, an effective proposal serves as an author's guide to developing, continuing, and completing the work on his or her book. From the outset, the very process of developing a proposal compels an author to focus beyond the idea of publishing a book and to form a realistic plan for organizing and performing the necessary work. Developing a proposal also requires that an author maps out the presentation of his or her book in a manner that makes sense for the given subject matter, and in a fashion that is understandable, meaningful, and attractive to publishers and to a targeted readership. Finally, a proposal serves as an ongoing guide and reminder to keep an author focused on the necessary pace and trajectory the book; this is crucial for writing projects that ordinarily take one to two years to complete.

Proposal Requirements. Most LIS publishers require the following core elements in book proposals that they receive:

- Proposed title and thorough description of the book.
- Detailed outline, including organization and full descriptions of sections and chapters.
- Thorough explanation of the significance and uniqueness of the subject matter.
- Target audience.
- Potential sales.
- Complete and relevant author qualifications.
- Estimated length of the manuscript in double-spaced, word-processed pages, including acknowledgements, preface, table of contents, references, figures, and appendices; estimated length of typeset book.
- Anticipated date of completion.

Most publishers will require that prospective authors provide a current résumé or curriculum vitae with their proposals. Some may require that authors include competitive analyses of similar books in or out of print, in development, or in press. Publishers may also stipulate that proposals include at least one completed section—a preface, an introduction, or a chapter. Conveniently, however, most LIS publishers facilitate the proposal process by providing online forms for authors to complete, or they give specific guidelines for authors to follow (see Appendix 1). There are no secrets in terms of the specific information publishers are looking for; it is incumbent on authors to present that information in a fashion that sells their ideas.

Editors. The model for reviewing book proposals varies slightly among LIS publishers, but it ordinarily involves a frontline person and a group of peer evaluators who report to him or her with comments, critiques, and suggestions. The frontline person commonly carries the title of editor, but he or she serves as both an editor and a liaison between the author and the publisher. Beyond these essential functions, the frontline person can also serve as a guide, a mentor, and even a proponent, particularly for newer or less experienced authors. The author's relationship with this person will have a major impact on authors' overall perceptions of the publishing experience. As Meyers (2003) wrote:

> Your publisher is important, but on a day-to-day basis, it is your editor who will make your life joyous or miserable. Your editor is your interface to the company, and if ever there were a time when a user-friendly interface were important, this is it. In my experience, your relationship with your editor will be the determining factor in your overall satisfaction in getting a book published. (para. 19)

Proposal Evaluators. Some LIS publishers rely on just one peer evaluator, but the norm is to have a group instead. Peer evaluators serve as an advisory group; they may even be recognized officially as a publisher's advisory board. Whatever their designation may be, the advisory group is comprised of knowledgeable and practiced LIS professionals who may or may not be affiliated with the publisher. More often than not, however, an advisory board is mainly comprised of professionals who are recruited from other institutions to lend their professional experience and disciplinary expertise to the proposal review process.

Proposal Review Process. In many respects the review process for book proposals is similar to the peer review process for scholarly papers, but there are some fundamental differences and distinctions. To begin, the format of a book requires that evaluators approach the proposal differently than they would a scholarly paper. The purpose of an LIS book is more functional in nature than an article in the discipline, and the scope is generally more comprehensive. Consequently, evaluators of book proposals must judge the relative utility and coverage of incomplete, potential works, as opposed to the success or failure of narrower arguments presented in completed papers. In terms of the actual reviews, book proposal evaluators are more likely to suggest larger changes in focus or direction for authors and publishers to consider, as opposed to specifying necessary revisions as a stipulation for acceptance. The mechanics of the review process are also different. Book proposals are commonly subjected to a single-blind review process in which evaluators are privy to proposing authors' names and credentials. This is different from the double-blind review process practiced by most LIS scholarly journals, but it is necessary for evaluators to judge whether or not authors have the appropriate expertise, experience, and writing skills for the works that they propose.

As a general rule, there are two levels of criteria that evaluators use when reviewing a book proposal. The first level of criteria involves the most fundamental considerations; evaluators will seek to determine whether or not authors satisfactorily address the core questions below. If the answer is "no" to any of these questions, the proposal will be rejected or returned to the author for necessary adjustments.

- Is the main idea for the book new or fresh?
- Is the main idea relevant for presentation in a book-length text?
- Will the main idea be of interest to readers?
- Does the author have the necessary experience or expertise to present the main idea?
- Does the author have the necessary writing skills to present the main idea?

The second level of evaluation criteria involves the more intricate details and subtleties of a book proposal; evaluators will seek to determine whether or not authors satisfactorily address the secondary questions below. If the answer is "no" to any of these questions, the proposal is unlikely to be rejected outright, but it will likely be returned to the author with recommendations for necessary adjustments.

- Does the author provide a sufficient amount of descriptive detail to project the idea of a successfully completed book?
- Are any elements of the author's main idea missing or misguided?
- Is the proposal organized in a manner that is logical, understandable, and useful to an intended readership of LIS professionals?

- Is the proposed style and tone appropriate for a book-length text and for an intended readership of LIS professionals?
- Is the proposed length and breadth appropriate for the main idea?

Some publishers give their evaluators a specified time period for reviewing proposals; four to six weeks is standard for book proposals in the social sciences. However, the business of publishing is competitive, even for LIS titles. As a result, the turnaround time for reviewing proposals is often expedited—one to two weeks is not uncommon. The rest of the review process unfolds very much like it does with scholarly papers that are submitted to journals for peer review. The evaluators report to the frontline person with their findings, and then the frontline person contacts the proposing author with a decision: accept, revise, resubmit, or reject. Library and information science publishers each have their own unique policies, practices, and preferences for administering evaluator reviews and for communicating the results to authors, but as a general rule, this is how the process works. Regardless of publishers' operations, however, the success or failure of any book idea depends on the effectiveness of the proposal. Even the most compelling book proposals are unlikely to be accepted if they are presented poorly.

Writing the Proposal

As noted, the proposal is the primary instrument used by authors to effectively communicate and sell their book writing ideas. Authors are encouraged to review the following suggestions for developing the strongest possible case for their proposals; they are also encouraged to review the Manuscript Preparation section of this text for practical reminders. Some of the recommendations and reminders below will come across as obvious procedures to the intended readership of LIS professionals; those same readers would likely be surprised to learn how many of their colleagues fail to abide by them.

- *Follow publisher instructions.* All LIS book publishers provide detailed guidelines for writing and submitting book proposals. Authors should view these guidelines as an opportunity to show publishers that they can follow instructions, and also that they can write well within those given parameters. The failure to follow publisher guidelines in any way is viewed unfavorably by editors and evaluators alike, and it dramatically increases the likelihood that a proposal will be rejected.

- ***Provide appropriate level of detail.*** Publishers and evaluators will require enough detail in a proposal to envision a book from start to finish; anything less will be dismissed as an underdeveloped idea. To that end, authors are encouraged to include an anticipated table of contents and a carefully crafted draft of a proposed section of the book. For the latter, an introduction or a preface may suffice, but a more substantial chapter is preferred. The sample section of the book is a key opportunity for authors to demonstrate their writing skills, their expertise in the main subject matter, and their commitment to the overall project. To the other extreme, authors are discouraged from submitting already completed books as proposals. As a matter of practicality, proposal evaluators are unlikely to have the time that is required to competently vet entire volumes, and it is not their responsibility to do so. Furthermore, publishers and evaluators may be inclined to regard already completed texts as undesirable works that are being shopped among, and perhaps rejected by other LIS publishers.
- ***Focus on the main topic or recurring theme.*** Authors must take great care to avoid straying off course with the presentation of their ideas in the proposal. The main topic or recurring theme of a text is the element that binds it together; that must be clearly evident in the proposal as well. Evaluators will want to see that authors remain diligently focused on the main topic throughout the proposal, that there are no gaps or loose ends, and also that the proposal is organized and presented in a manner that is logical for the given subject matter.
- ***Include design hooks.*** It is prudent for authors to include attractive, useful, or unique elements of design, or "design hooks," in the proposal. Design hooks do much to enhance the appeal of the proposal because they help evaluators to envision the completed work, and also to judge the value of that work in a more tangible sense. The possibilities of design hooks are far ranging, and even more so with electronic books, even though scholarly books are generally presented in a more

conservative manner. Still, examples of design hooks that authors might consider include icons, images, highlighting features, layout features, navigational aids, recommended exercises, sidebars, specific chapter structures, supplemental anecdotes, text callouts, theme-setting quotations, and vignettes.

- *Identify the market potential.* Market potential is commonly identified by publishers as the weakest area of book proposals in the social sciences. Publishers will always require that authors include specifics about targeted readership and potential sales in their proposals. It is not enough, however, for authors to simply claim that a proposed book is significant or unique, and that it will have appeal with a relevant audience of LIS professionals. Authors must endeavor to justify what they propose with compelling factual information. The nature of a proposed work will dictate which facts to include, but authors are generally encouraged to abide by the following rules:

  » *Persuasive details.* Authors must go beyond simply describing the significance and noteworthiness of their proposed work; they must clearly demonstrate these assertions. This is ordinarily accomplished by conducting a comprehensive literature review, by comparing and contrasting with other works on the same subject matter, and by identifying gaps or trends in the discipline or practice that make the proposal timely and relevant. Authors will need to map out these details and cite any relevant sources; this is required evidence in support of the proposal. It should be noted, however, that the authority and credibility of any cited sources will also have an impact on the persuasiveness of the proposal. Evaluators are particularly skilled at detecting weakly supported assertions.

  » *Statistics.* Authors must provide appropriate statistics in support of their proposal assertions. Although the nature of the proposal may require the use of other supporting numbers, the most germane statistics will relate to projected book sales, competing book sales, and targeted audiences. Statistics for scholarly book sales can be a challenge to retrieve, and thus to predict; the former is proprietary information and the latter is speculative and imprecise. Still, authors can use the *WorldCat* database to retrieve a reasonably accurate number of libraries that own competing books, factoring that this does not account for institutions with multiple copies or for the limited number of copies that are purchased for personal or professional use. Next, authors can use statistics available through professional association reports to reasonably estimate the size of their target audience. The American Library Association's annual *State of America's Libraries Report* is freely accessible on the web, and it includes current statistics for all its divisions and for all types of practicing librarians. With these two sets of numbers—competing books sales and size of target audience—authors can make reasonable sales estimations for their proposed work.

- *Prepare to write well.* As noted, the proposal is an opportunity for authors to demonstrate their writing skills—that is, their ability to write clearly, compellingly, logically, grammatically correct, and in an appropriate style and tone for the format and the given subject matter. For this reason, authors are strongly encouraged to review the Elements of Writing Well chapter of this text and to refer to it and other authoritative writing and style guides habitually.
- *Have a colleague review.* Selecting an appropriate colleague to review one's proposal is vitally important. Another LIS professional's perspective is necessary for making certain that one's work is effectively presented, and also for catching errors in flow, logic, and mechanics that an author may have overlooked. The colleague selected should be an experienced author, a skilled writer and editor, and an honest reviewer (i.e., willing to provide all necessary criticisms). Additionally, that person should be knowledgeable about the subject matter of an author's proposal, and he or she should be well-versed in the related professional literature.

6.3 *Publisher Decision*

The frontline person or editor will contact proposing authors with the publisher decision to accept or reject a book proposal, or to recommend or require certain revisions. Authors are encouraged to review the Manuscript Decisions section of this text for recommendations on how they should respond to the publisher decision; responding to publisher decisions on scholarly book proposals is highly comparable to responding to editorial decisions on scholarly papers. However, it is important to reiterate a few points here, and to emphasize some new ones that are unique to book proposals:

- Proposed books always involve more work than authors initially anticipate.
- Publisher decisions will always include recommended or required adjustments.
- Editor and evaluator comments almost always include ideas that authors had not considered or information that authors did not know.
- All editor and evaluator comments should be seriously considered and then addressed in one manner or another.
- Recommended or required adjustments should be addressed immediately; the proposal must be prioritized.
- Recommended or required adjustments can be negotiated between the author and the editor.
- Editor and evaluator comments are not personal attacks; respond professionally.
- Regardless of the publisher's decision on the proposal, respond promptly.
- The nature of editor and evaluator comments may dictate whether or not authors should continue working with the same publisher or consider resubmitting elsewhere.
- There is more than one LIS book publisher; all scholars experience rejection.
- Proposed books are sometimes, for one reason or another, unlikely to be accepted for publication anywhere; the nature of editor and evaluator comments may make this clear; be accepting of this possibility,

and be thankful that one to two years of work will not go to waste on an unpublishable text.

Contracts

Assuming that a book proposal is ultimately accepted, publishers will issue a contract, a memorandum of understanding (MOU), or a memorandum of agreement (MOA) for authors to sign. These documents are characteristically presented in lengthy, stodgy, and even intimidating legalese. Authors may benefit from consulting with a legal professional before signing, but in the context of the scholarly LIS book, it is often unnecessary to do so. The intended readership for this text is comprised of professionals who are skilled at finding, synthesizing, and effectively using new or unfamiliar information. If authors are sophisticated enough to develop and write a scholarly book, then they should be perfectly equipped to deal with a contract or MOU/MOA on this modest scale.

The most commonly concerning terms of the LIS book contract or MOU/MOA are related to copyright ownership, rights, permissions, and royalties from sales. However, the contemporary book marketplace requires that authors and publishers consider and negotiate other related details—electronic book options, institutional repositories, open access, and print-on-demand services, to name a few. The operative term is "negotiate," because publishers are flexible on most terms. Still, authors should be realistic about their wishes; book publishing is ultimately a business, and publishers will not agree to unreasonable, unworthy, or unprofitable terms.

Copyright. The standard book contract or MOU/MOA will ordinarily stipulate that the copyright is to be registered in the publisher's name. Authors may or may not have strong feelings about this; most LIS professionals do. As a result, most LIS publishers have alternative contracts or MOUs/MOAs that allow for authors to maintain full ownership of their work. This may not be a critical point in the context of scholarly LIS books because the contract or MOU/MOA will always include the necessary protections for publishers' business interests, because publishers are generally amenable to granting authors whatever reasonable permissions they may want or need, and because copyright ownership is unlikely to make any significant difference one way or another in terms of publisher revenues or author royalties.

Rights. In simple terms, the contract or MOU/MOA will state that an author gives a publisher the rights to print, publish, reproduce, distribute, and vend his or her work in all formats, and that the publisher is required to compensate the author according to other agreed-upon terms and conditions. Authors will want to be certain that those rights revert back to them after an agreed upon length of time, or once their work is discontinued or reaches an agreed upon point of sales inactivity. The inclusion of the latter two rights will require negotiation because the relative ease of storing electronic files and the ubiquity of print-on-demand services in the publishing marketplace means that books rarely go out-of-print anymore. These rights are particularly important for LIS professionals who ultimately intend to upload open access versions of their work to the web or to their institutional repositories. The contract or MOU/MOA may also include provisional rights to address the potential for subsequent, new editions; publishers will want the right to demand new editions and to solicit a new writer if the original author declines. For their part, authors will want the right to either accept or decline the publisher's first offer for a new edition.

Permissions. As noted, LIS publishers are generally amenable to including any reasonable permissions in the contract or MOU/MOA, but these will need to be negotiated. Authors should look to identify those terms and conditions that may prevent them from accomplishing what they wish to with their work. Authors may wish, for instance, to use significant portions of their work for the purposes of presenting, teaching, or conducting research. Most LIS publishers will understand that these professional activities increases visibility, and as a result, they generally boost sales as well. Authors may also wish to post a pre or post-publication versions of their book in an institutional repository. In due course, all publishers will come to understand that this is a sound business practice, but to date, not all publishers are currently amenable.

Royalties. As noted, LIS authors are unlikely to realize great wealth from sales of their work. Crawford (2003) suggested that "two thousand copies represent good sales in the library market" (p. 82), but achieving that number of scholarly LIS book sales is highly optimistic. The sale of five hundred copies is generally regarded as a successful, scholarly LIS publication. Library science textbooks are a common exception to this rule, though not all of those works result in significantly greater sales. As emphasized throughout the course of this text, the purpose of academic writing is to contribute something new to the professional discourse; the chief concerns of authors should be writing well, and then having their work packaged professionally and disseminated to the broadest possible swath of potential readers. If authors successfully execute their end of the bargain, then publishers have the established mechanisms in place to package and disseminate the final product, and the resulting sales will be driven by demand in the LIS marketplace.

Library and information science publishers commence paying royalties to authors after the expenses for production are fully recouped. Some publishers will provide very modest advances when the contract or MOU/MOA is signed, but those payments are simply advances on anticipated royalties. As a general rule, most LIS titles will require about 200 sales to recoup production expenses, after which authors are typically paid 10-15 percent of the net receipts for additional sales. These numbers will vary from publisher to publisher, but not significantly.

Format. Given the evolving landscape of scholarly communication, it is advantageous for authors and publishers alike to negotiate contracts that include the production of books in print and also in a variety of possible electronic formats. The continuing popularity of print books among LIS professionals is indisputable, and that will continue to be true for the foreseeable future. At the same time, electronic editions are becoming more functional and widespread, and thus, more important to the work of practitioners, educators, and researchers. All major LIS publishers offer electronic books, and an increasing percentage of those publishers' catalogs are either available through bundled subscriptions or they are carried by major aggregators like Ebook Library, Ebrary, Ebsco, and MyiLibrary. At present, it is unnecessary to produce or format electronic LIS texts specifically for reader devices like Kindle, Nook, or Sony Reader. Although their proprietary reader applications are downloadable and interoperable, they remain somewhat limiting in terms of access, and they are generally inappropriate for scholarly texts. It should be noted, however, that the ePub format—the open web electronic book standard—is readable among all devices, and it is increasingly adopted by LIS publishers for individual book sales. Furthermore, popular reader devices have essentially become computing tablets; newer generations of these devices allow users to access electronic texts on the web, and this is likely to have a significant impact on the scholarly marketplace.

Authors are also encouraged to negotiate with their publishers for potential open access versions of their work. It is not unprecedented for ACRL, for instance, to agree to the release of open access editions after an agreed upon length of time following the original releases of corresponding print editions. It may seem counterintuitive at first, but progressive publishers will eventually recognize that the increased visibility that comes by way of open access is a sagacious strategy for generating increased sales.

6.4 Book Writing Advice, Recommendations, and Strategies

Once a contract or MOU/MOA is finalized and signed, authors should be properly positioned to commence working on their book without any further procedural distractions. Given that authors will be responsible for delivering a completed manuscript to their publisher based on the time table in their accepted proposal, it is vital that they have a realistic plan for conducting the necessary work. Regardless of one's writing and publishing experience, this requires an exceptional level of commitment, discipline, and strategy. Authors are encouraged to heed the following recommended preparations, processes, and practicalities for the purpose of successfully completing the book-length manuscript, and for delivering it to their publisher in a timely manner.

Writing Preparations
Organize supporting materials. Authors should organize their supporting research materials, whether print or electronic, in a manner that reflects the anticipated development of their book. The simplest, and perhaps

most sensible method is to organize one's research materials around the book's anticipated table of contents. Authors who prefer to retrieve and maintain their supporting materials electronically—including the use of bibliographic management software—are recommended to create separate folders for different chapters or sections of their book, or as necessary, for different types of materials. Importantly, however, the selected method of organization must be flexible; authors will need to add new works, remove those that become irrelevant, and reorganize to accommodate inevitable changes in a book's development.

Keep reference materials at hand at all times. Experienced authors already do this as a matter of good habit, but it is important to reiterate the importance of keeping print copies of one's preferred writing style guide, dictionary, thesaurus, and grammar text in their work space at all times. These reference materials are increasingly available on the free web and by way of popular word processing applications, but to date the electronic versions remain less authoritative, less robust, and less reliable than the familiar, print texts.

Establish a productive routine. It may not always be possible, but authors should identify a part of the day in which they are consistently energetic and productive, and they should try to establish their writing routine to take advantage that time. Whether it is a specific time of day, or specific days of the week, establishing a stable writing routine is critical for generating and maintaining momentum, and that momentum is necessary for completing book-length projects.

Writing Processes

Focus on one small task at a time. Writing a book is an enormous task. It can be overwhelming to the point of being counterproductive for authors to contemplate the overall text and the work that is necessary to complete it. Hundreds of working sessions are required for completing book-length writing projects. Authors must be focused solely on the quality of one small section of the text during each session, and they must train themselves to write within this mindset. The combination of maintaining a necessary focus and adhering to an established routine are the key determinants for making significant progress on any book project.

Begin each writing session by reviewing the work from the previous one. Constant editing, reorganizing, and reworking are necessary processes for any writing project. Authors should plan to include these processes in their established writing routine by beginning each session with a review of their previous session's work. This gives authors the opportunity to read and revise their previous work with a fresher perspective, it helps to improve the organization and the logical flow of an author's work through more effective transitions, and it establishes the necessary momentum for each new writing session.

Finish each writing session with an incomplete thought. It is a greater challenge for authors to be productive when they are consistently beginning their writing sessions with unbroached subject matter. To facilitate a quicker and more seamless transition into the writing process, authors should make a habit of finishing their writing sessions with incomplete thoughts, or even incomplete sentences. This helps authors to enter into subsequent sessions with effective mental bookmarks, and also with a greater sense of momentum.

Capture ideas that emerge when not in writing sessions. It is a common experience for authors to cogitate about their writing projects when otherwise occupied by surface-level daily activities—bathing, cooking, driving, exercising, trying to fall asleep—and it is vitally important to capture any pertinent ideas that might materialize. New ideas that emerge in circumstances outside of writing sessions can prove to be pivotal, but they can also be fleeting. Authors should be prepared at all times to immediately document new ideas by whatever means are most practical.

Be flexible to inevitable and necessary changes. The form of a scholarly book can be predicted to a reasonable degree in the proposal, but as authors are writing, they are cautioned to avoid the imposition of a predetermined structure might minimize the impact of the subject matter. As a book-length writing project is developed, it will require constant reevaluation and reorganization. The course of the subject matter will inevitably stray from the original outline as mapped out in the proposal; this is normal. Necessary changes will become apparent as authors seek to establish a coherent and logical flow among sections of their work. As long as authors maintain their focus, the subject matter will dictate the proper form and organization of the text. The table of contents can always be rewritten.

Be accepting of the time that is required. Authors enter into book writing projects with very specific intentions in terms of what they wish to communicate and how. However, the writing process is an exercise in discovery; authors will invariably encounter new and unanticipated ideas about the main subject matter and how those ideas should be communicated. Although most experienced authors will try to account for the process of discovery in their proposals, the actual development of their work will almost always require more time than that which is originally projected.

Take a day off. As noted, writing a book requires an exceptional level of commitment and discipline. However, the more times an author reads over the same sentences, passages, or paragraphs, the more likely it is that he or she will miss subtle, or even obvious errors in flow, logic, and mechanics. While it is true that a hard push of diligence is required to fully prepare a book manuscript for submission, it is also true that a rested and refreshed author will catch and correct more writing errors. Authors are highly encouraged to occasionally take a day or more away from their manuscript in order to recharge, and to spend that time focused on other, unrelated matters.

Have a colleague review. Selecting an appropriate colleague to review one's work is vitally important. Another LIS professional's perspective is necessary for making certain that one's work is effectively argued and presented, and also for catching errors in flow, logic, and mechanics that an author may have overlooked. The colleague selected should be an experienced author, a skilled writer and editor, and an honest reviewer (i.e., willing to provide all necessary criticisms). Additionally, that person should be knowledgeable about the subject matter of an author's manuscript, and he or she should be well-versed in the related professional literature.

Edit, revise, and proofread again. After fully considering their colleagues' comments and criticisms, authors should make the changes they deem to be necessary for the betterment of their work. Even the most experienced and polished LIS authors will need to revise their work, particularly with book-length writing projects. Although manuscript fatigue is common and understandable at this point of a book's development, authors must summon the necessary fortitude to make any necessary revisions, and then they are recommended, once again, to take a day off before one or two final proof readings.

Writing Practicalities

Maintain separate documents for different chapters or sections of the book.
It is common for authors to quickly fall into the trap of developing a book in just one or two lengthy manuscript documents. Such documents quickly become unwieldy; they are difficult to maintain and even more difficult to reorganize. Authors are highly encouraged to create separate documents for different chapters or sections of their manuscript. As with the recommended organization of supporting research materials, the simplest, and perhaps most sensible method is to create separate documents for each discrete chapter or section that is identified in the book's anticipated table of contents. Ultimately, most LIS publishers will want authors to submit their completed work in this manner instead of in one or two colossal documents.

Back up the work often, and in multiple locations. Every reader of this text has received or even issued this warning numerous times, and still, most have lost minor or major parts of their work to electronic glitches or malfunctions. Hard drives crash, servers go down, files become corrupt, and viruses are ever-present. It is absolutely essential, not only to habitually back up one's work often, but also to do so in multiple locations.

6.5 Advice, Recommendations, and Strategies for Edited Volumes

There are several unique elements to developing edited volumes that require additional guidance. Clearly, those who are responsible for developing these volumes must be skilled readers, editors, and writers, but it is equally true that book editors must be effective communicators and capable administrators, and that they must have sound work flow strategies in place. Book editors do not have the luxury of self-reliance; they are forced to rely on the contributions of other authors, and that poses a unique set of challenges. For this reason, editors are recommended to heed the following recommendations.

- Plan to be the author of at least one chapter or significant section of the text.

- Prepare self-authored chapters or sections for inclusion in the book proposal, and also for the purpose of soliciting other high-caliber contributors.
- Solicit contributions directly from known scholars or colleagues in the profession who are already published authors, and who are proven experts in relevant subject matter.
- Conduct a literature review to identify additional scholars in the profession who are already published authors, and who are proven experts in relevant subject matter.
- Solicit additional contributors, when necessary, through networking and relevant professional discussion lists.
- Include the following in any contributor solicitations: the proposed book title, a concise description, the intended publisher, the projected timeline for stages of the book, and the expected date of publication.
- Require that unknown, proposing contributors provide current curricula vitae and/or bibliographies of previous publications.
- Thoroughly vet the curricula vitae and/or previous publications of proposing contributors.
- Require that unpublished, proposing contributors provide a professional writing sample.
- Reject contributor proposals that include any unprofessional content or evidence of unsatisfactory writing skills.
- Provide reasonable, but firm deadlines for potential contributors to submit proposals, and for accepted contributors to submit first and final drafts of their work; enforce those deadlines.
- Provide potential and accepted contributors with reasonable, but firm editorial deadlines; abide by those deadlines.
- Provide accepted contributors with exacting guidelines for chapter content, format, style, tone, and length.
- Have the courage to remove noncompliant and ineffective authors, even if their contributions have already been tentatively accepted or agreed upon.
- Provide contributors and publishers with timely updates on the development of the book.
- Operate in a manner that is completely transparent to contributors and publishers.

Benefits of the Edited Book

Notwithstanding the challenges indicated by the bullet list of recommendations above, editing a volume of collected papers has the potential to be a uniquely rewarding undertaking. To begin, it is a productive way of connecting with other scholars in one's field. As noted, book editors are encouraged to solicit contributed works from leaders in their field; those scholars may not always be able to commit to one's book project, but they may have useful ideas to share, and the simple act of communicating with them is in and of itself an exercise that often generates future benefits. Editing a volume of collected papers also provides the opportunity to collaborate with colleagues who one truly desires to work with; this can make for a particularly gratifying scholarly experience. Finally, editing a book continues to be a valuable endeavor for advancing disciplinary discourse, and it is an effective way of establishing, bolstering, or solidifying one's reputation in his or her field.

Chapter 6 Appendix

Association of College & Research Libraries Publication Proposal

1. Working title: _____

2. Expected publication date: _____

3. Estimated length of completed manuscript: _____

4. Attach a summary of the content/size/approach of this publication (approximately 50 words).

5. Attach an outline of the proposed publication. Be as specific about the content as possible (e.g., chapter headings, articles, titles, authors, introduction, etc.).

6. What will be the tone and style of the publication?

7. In approximately 25 words, explain why this book differs from other books on the same subject.

8. What is the significance of this publication?

9. Define the target audience for this publication. Provide information about the potential market for this publication, including the number of people you estimate might purchase the publication from each group.

10. Provide information about the author(s) showing his/her qualifications for writing this work. A resume or vita may be attached.

11. Who will be responsible for coordinating the development of this publication?

    Name _____

    Address _____

    Phone No _____

    E-mail _____

Association of College & Research Libraries Publication Proposal, cont.

12. Who will be asked to review the material prior to final submission? Give name, address, telephone number, and pertinent expertise.

13. Other comments:

Person Submitting This Form

Name: _____

ACRL Section: _____

Committee: _____

Address: _____

Telephone: (H) _____ (W) _____

Date: _____

**Please save and return form and related materials to
Kathryn Deiss at kdeiss@ala.org[1]**

Concluding Notes

Academic writing is an exceptionally worthwhile and valuable enterprise. When done well, scholarly LIS writing is beneficial to authors in terms of professional achievement and fulfillment; it is instructive and inspirational to readers; it advances disciplinary discourse; and it has the ultimate potential of improving professional practice. As with most scholarly endeavors, however, the relative impact and success of academic writing is not random or serendipitous; real achievement is gained through a necessary sequence of forming ideas, asking relevant questions, developing and testing hypotheses, conducting research, assessing outcomes, and presenting arguments to appropriate audiences. All of these steps involve practical elements that authors must learn to master—writing effectively; structuring a strong and coherent scholarly argument; choosing a suitable medium; selecting an appropriate publisher or publication; and presenting in a manner that balances the nature of the subject matter, the norms of the medium, and the needs and expectations of the publisher, the publication, and the audience. These are the elements that distinguish between effective and ineffective scholarly communication, and improving them has been the focus of this handbook.

Readers of this text are reminded that academic writing is an honorable undertaking with rich historical traditions, but it need not be an exercise in stodgy or turgid scholarship. On the contrary, when done well, academic writing can be an elegant and illuminating form of scholarly expression. Academic writing is a craft, a discipline, and most importantly, it is an acquired skill. The necessary elements of this type of writing are learned over time; they are developed and honed through hard work; they are refined by editorial criticism; and they are molded by professional experience and profuse experimentation and application. Implicit to all this is the fact that authors, themselves, are responsible for improving their own writing skills, and furthermore, for choosing where and how to publish their works. Authors must *want* to be better writers, to publish in appropriate places, and to contribute to the literature in a meaningful fashion.

Notes and References

Notes

Chapter 2: Elements of the Scholarly Paper
1. Permission was granted by the authors, Peg Cook and Mary Barbara Walsh, to include their complete literature review in this text.

Chapter 4: Elements of Selecting the Right Journal
1. Statistics retrieved from a search of the *Ulrich's International Periodicals Directory* database, March 14, 2012, and then reconfirmed December 31, 2012.
2. Statistics retrieved from a search of the *WorldCat* database, March 15, 2012, and then reconfirmed December 31, 2012.
3. Search executed in the *Library & Information Science Full Text* database, March 22, 2012, and then reconfirmed December 31, 2012.
4. Search executed in the *Cabell's Directory of Publishing Opportunities in Educational Technology and Library Science* database, April 2, 2012, and then reconfirmed December 31, 2012.
5. Information gleaned from the *LIS Publications Wiki* on April 4, 2012, and then reconfirmed on December 31, 2012.
6. Information gleaned from the *LIS Publications Wiki* on April 5, 2012, and then reconfirmed on December 31, 2012.
7. Search executed in the 2010 edition of the *Journal Citation Reports* database, March 21, 2012. (Note: The 2011 edition of the same database shows an impact factor of 2.146 for the journal, *Information Systems Research*.)
8. Statistics retrieved from a search of the *Ulrich's International Periodicals Directory* database, March 20, 2012, and then reconfirmed January 2, 2013.
9. Search executed in the 2010 edition of the *Journal Citation Reports* database, March 27, 2012. (Note: The 2011 edition of the same database does not include a ranking for the journal, *Journal of the American Informatics Association*.)

10. Search executed in the *SCImago Journal & Country Rank* database, January 2, 2012.
11. Search executed in the *Directory of Open Access Journals* database, January 2, 2012.

Chapter 5: Elements of the Publishing Process

1. Permission was granted by the authors, Janet Goosney and Christopher Hollister, to include the full text of their "Reviewer Guidelines for *Communication in Information Literacy* (CIL)" as an appendix in this text. (Note: Authors for CIL retain full ownership of their work under a *Creative Commons* copyright agreement. Notwithstanding this fact, the reviewer guidelines for CIL are also reprinted in this text with the approval of the journal's editors.)

Chapter 6: Elements of the Scholarly Book

1. Permission was granted by the publisher, Association of College & Research Libraries, to include the full text of their web-based "Publication Proposal" form as an appendix in this text.

References

Abrikosov, A., Agre, P, Berg, P, Bishop, J., Buck, L., Chalfie, M., …Watson, J. (2012). An open letter to the U.S. Congress signed by 52 Nobel Prize winners. Retrieved from http://www.arl.org/sparc/bm~doc/2012-nobelists-lofgren.pdf

American Library Association. (2011). Number employed in libraries. Retrieved from http://www.ala.org/tools/libfactsheets/alalibraryfactsheet02

American Psychological Association. (2010). *Publication Manual of the American Psychological Association* (6th ed.). Washington, DC: American Psychological Association.

Association for Library Collections and Technical Services. (2012). For LRTS Authors. Retrieved from http://www.ala.org/alcts/resources/lrts/authfaq

Association of American Universities. (2009). The university's role in the dissemination of research and scholarship – A call to action. Retrieved from http://www.arl.org/bm~doc/disseminating-research-feb09.pdf

Association of College & Research Libraries. (2013, March).Selective list of journals on teaching & learning. Retrieved from http://www.ala.org/acrl/aboutacrl/directoryofleadership/sections/is/iswebsite/projpubs/journalsteachinglearning

Association of College & Research Libraries. (n.d.). Publication proposal. Retrieved from http://www.ala.org/acrl/sites/ala.org.acrl/files/content/resources/forms/prlmpub.pdf

Banks, M, & Dellavalle, R. (2008). Emerging alternatives to the impact factor. *OCLC Systems & Services 24*(3): 167-173.

Barendse, W. (2007). The strike rate index: A new index for journal quality based on journal size and the h-index of citations. *Biomedical Digital Libraries 4*(3). Retrieved from http://www.bio-diglib.com/content/4/1/3

Bauer, S. (1984). Ethics (or lack thereof) of refereeing. *Chemical & Engineering News, 62*(52): 2, 33.

Beck, S., & Manuel, K. (2004). *Practical Research Methods for Librarians and Information Professionals.* New York: Neal-Schuman.

Belcher, W. (2009). *Writing your journal article in 12 weeks: A guide to academic publishing success.* Thousand Oaks, CA: Sage Publications.

Bergstrom, C. (2007, May). Eigenfactor: Measuring the value and prestige of scholarly journals. *College and Research Libraries News 68*: 314-316.

Bergstrom, T., & McAfee, P. (2005). An open letter to all university presidents and provosts concerning increasingly expensive journals. Retrieved from http://www.mcafee.cc/Journal/OpenLetter.pdf

Best, R., & Kneip, J. (2010). Library school programs and the successful training of academic librarians to meet promotion and tenure requirements in the academy. *College & Research Libraries 71*(2): 97-114.

Blake, V. (1996). The perceived prestige of professional journals, 1995: A replication of the Kohl-Davis study. *Education for Information 14*(3): 157-179.

Bowles-Terry, M., Hensley, M., & Hinchliffe, L. (2010). Best practices for online video tutorials in academic libraries: A study of student preferences and understanding. *Communications in Information Literacy 4*(1), 17-28. Retrieved from http://comminfolit.org/index.php?journal=cil&page=article&op=viewFile&path%5B%5D=Vol4-2010AR1&path%5B%5D=112

Brown, H. (1972). History and the learned journal. *Journal of the History of Ideas 33*(3), Festschrift for Philip P. Wieners: pp. 365-378.

Budd, J. (2001). Information seeking in theory and practice: Rethinking public services in libraries. *Reference & User Services Quarterly, 40*(3), 256-263.

Budden, A., Tregenza, T., Aarssen, L., Koricheva, J., Leimu, R., & Lortie, C. (2008). Double-blind review favours increased representation of female authors. *Trends in Ecology & Evolution, 23*(1): 4-6. doi: 10.1016/j.tree.2007.07.008

Campanario, J. (1996). Have referees rejected some of the most-cited articles of all times? *Journal of the American Society for Information Science, 47*(4): 302-310.

Communications in Information Literacy. (2012). Retrieved from http://www.comminfolit.org

Consolidated Appropriations Act of 2008, Pub. L. No. 110-161, § 218, 121 Stat. (2008).

Cook, P., & Walsh, M. (2012). Collaboration and problem-based learning: Integrating information literacy into a political science course. *Communications in Information Literacy*, 6(1): 59-72. Retrieved from http://www.comminfolit.org

Crawford, W. (2003). *First have something to say: Writing for the library profession*. Chicago: American Library Association.

Davis, P. (2008). Eigenfactor: Does the principle of repeated improvement result in better estimates than raw citation counts? *Journal of the American Society of Information Science and Technology* 59(13): 2186-2188. doi: 10.1002/asi.20943

Elsevier. (2012). Elsevier Editorial System (EES). Retrieved from http://www.elsevier.com/wps/find/editorshome.editors/Onlinesubmission

Emerald. (2012). Library Hi Tech information | Author Guidelines. Retrieved from http://www.emeraldinsight.com/products/journals/author_guidelines.htm

Eysenbach, G. (2006). Citation advantage of open access articles. *PLoS Biology* 4(5): e157.doi:10.1371/journal.pbio.0040157

Federal Research Public Access Act of 2012, S. 2096, 112th Cong. 2d Sess (2012).

Fister, B. (2007). Foreword. *Communications in Information Literacy* 1(1-2): i.

Garvey, W., Lin, N., & Tomita, K. (1972). Research studies in patterns of scientific communication: III. Information-exchange processes associated with the production of journal articles. *Information Storage and Retrieval*, 8(5): 207-221.

Goosney, J., & Hollister, C. (2009). Reviewer Guidelines for Communications in Information Literacy. Retrieved from http://www.comminfolit.org/index.php?journal=cil

Grant, B. (2010, June 21). New impact factors yield surprise. *The Scientist*. Retrieved from http://classic.the-scientist.com/blog/display/57500/

Harvard University. (2008, February 19). Harvard University unanimously votes 'yes' for open access. Retrieved from http://cyber.law.harvard.edu/node/3927

Hendrix, D. (2010). Relationships between Association of Research Libraries (ARL) statistics and bibliometric indicators: A principal components analysis. *College & Research Libraries* 71(1): 32-41.

Henry, A., & Roseberry, R. (1997). An investigation of the functions, strategies, and linguistic features of the introductions and conclusions of essays. *System* 25(4): 479-495.

Hernon, P., & Metoyer-Duran, C. (1993). Problem statements: An exploratory study of their function, significance, and form. *Library and Information Science Research 15*(1): 71-92.

Hernon, P., Smith, A., & Croxen, M. (1993). Publication in *College & Research Libraries*: Accepted, rejected, and published papers, 1980-1991. *College & Research Libraries 54*(4): 303-321.

Hirsch, J. (2005). An index to quantify an individual's scientific research output. *Proceedings of the National Academy of Sciences 102*(46): 16569-16572. doi: 10.1073/pnas.0507655102

Hollister, C. (2001). Price inflation and discrimination extends to non-STM disciplines: A study of library and information science journals. *Current Studies in Librarianship 25*(1-2): 49-57.

Hoorn, E. (2005, October 30). Repositories, copyright and Creative Commons for scholarly communication. *Ariadne 45*. Retrieved from http://www.ariadne .ac.uk/issue45/hoorn

Johns Hopkins University Press. (2012). portal: Libraries and the Academy. Retrieved from http://www.press.jhu.edu/journals/portal_libraries_and _the_academy/guidelines.html

Kern, M., & Hensley, M. (2011). Citation management software: Features and futures. *Reference & User Services Quarterly, 50*(3), 204-208.

Kohl, D., & Davis, C. (1985). Rating of journals by ARL library directors and deans of library and information science schools. *College & Research Libraries 46*(1): 40-47.

Laband, D., & Piette, M. (1994). A citation analysis of the impact of blinded peer review. *Journal of the American Medical Association, 272*(2): 147-149. doi: 10.1001/jama.272.2.147

Lazonder, A. W., Hagemans, M. G., & de Jong, T. (2010). Offering and discovering domain information in simulation-based inquiry learning. *Learning & Instruction, 20*(6), 511-520. doi:10.1016/j.learninstruc.2009.08.001

Library and Information Science Editors. (2012). Guide to Best Practices for Editors of Library and Information Science Journals. Retrieved from http://www.lis-editors.org/best-practices/index.shtml

Long, D. (2011). Latino students' perceptions of the academic library. *Journal of Academic Librarianship 37*(6): 504-511.

Loubert, L., & Nelson, F. (2010). The impact of collective bargaining and urbanicity on the late hiring of teachers. *Leadership & Policy in Schools, 9*(4), 421-440. doi:10.1080/15700760903342384

Manten, A. (1980). Development of European scientific journal publishing before 1850. In A.J.

Meadows (Ed.), *Development of Science Publishing in Europe* (pp. 1-22). New York: Elsevier Science.

McAllister-Harper, D. (1993). An analysis of courses in cataloging and classification and related areas offered in sixteen graduate library schools and their relationship to present and future trends in cataloging and classification and to cognitive needs of professional academic catalogers. *Cataloging & Classification Quarterly* 16(3): 99-123.

McGrath, W. (2002). Introduction. *Library Trends* 50(3): 309-316.

McKechnie, L., & Pettigrew, K. (2002). Surveying the use of theory in library and information science research: A disciplinary perspective. *Library Trends* 50(3): 406-417.

Medical Library Association. (January, 2013). Journal of the Medical Library Association: Instructions for Authors. Retrieved from http://www.mlanet .org/publications/jmla/jmlainfo.html#writing

Meho, L., & Yang, K. (2007). Impact of data sources on citation counts and rankings of LIS faculty: web of Science versus Scopus and Google Scholar. *Journal of the American Society of Information Science and Technology* 58(13): 2105-2125. doi: 10.1002/asi.20677

Meyers, S. (2003). Advice to prospective book authors. Retrieved from http://www.aristeia.com/authorAdvice.html

Mi, M. (2011). Renewed roles for librarians in problem-based learning in the medical curriculum. *Medical Reference Services Quarterly,* 30(3), 269-282.

Miksa, F. (1988). The Columbia School of Library Economy, 1887-1888. *Libraries & Culture* 23(3): 249-280.

Monastersky, R. (2005, March 14). The number that's devouring science. *Chronicle of Higher Education* 52(8). Retrieved from http://www.chronicle.com

Nadiri, H., & Mayboudi, S. (2010). Diagnosing university students' zone of tolerance from university library services. *Malaysian Journal of Library & Information Science* 15(1): 1-21.

Nisonger, T., & Davis, C. (2005). The perception of library and information science journals by LIS education deans and ARL library directors: A replication of the Kohl-Davis study. *College & Research Libraries* 66(4): 341-377.

Open Citation Project. (2012). The effect of open access and downloads ('hits') on citation impact: A bibliography of studies. Retrieved from http://opcit .eprints.org/oacitation-biblio.html

Pettigrew, K., & McKechnie, L. (2001). The use of theory in information science research. *Journal of the American Society for Information Science and Technology* 52(1): 62-73.

Portal: Libraries and the Academy. (2012). Author Guidelines. Retrieved from https://www.press.jhu.edu/journals/portal_libraries_and_the_academy/ guidelines.html

Pritchard, S. (2012). Double-blind review: A commitment to fair editorial practices. *portal: Libraries and the Academy, 12*(2): 117-119. doi: 10.1353/pla.2012.0022

Public Knowledge Project. (2012). Open Journal Systems. Retrieved from http://pkp.sfu.ca/?q=ojs

Ross, J., Gross, C., Desai, M., Hong, Y., Grant, A., Daniels, S., … Krumholz, H. (2006). Effect of blinded peer review on abstract acceptance. *Journal of the American Medical Association, 295*(14): 1675-1680. doi: 10.1001/jama.295.14.1675

Rossner, M., Van Epps, H., & Hill, E. (2007). Show me the data. *Journal of Cell Biology 179*(6): 1091-1092. doi: 10.1083/jcb.200711140

Rotton, J., Foos, P., Van Meek, L., & Levitt, M. (1995). Publication practices and the file drawer problem. *Journal of Social Behavior and Personality, 10*(1): 1-13.

Schlimgen, J., & Kronefeld, M. (2004). Update on inflation of journal prices: Brandon/Hill list journals and the scientific, technical, and medical publishing market. *Journal of the Medical Library Association 92*(3): 307-314.

Shelly II, M., & Mack, C. (2001). Are the best higher education journals really the best? A meta-analysis of writing quality and readability. *Journal of Scholarly Publishing 33*(1): 11-22.

Shera, J. (1976). *Introduction to Library Science*. Littleton, CO: Libraries Unlimited.

Simon, C. (2011). Just the facts: An examination of e-book usage by business students and faculty. *The Reference Librarian 52*(3): 263-273.

Simon, R., Bakanic, V, & McPhail, C. (1986). Who complains to journal editors and what happens. *Sociological Inquiry, 56*(2): 259-271.

Smale. M., & Regaldo, M. (2009). Using Blackboard to deliver library research skills assessment: A case study. *Communications in Information Literacy 3*(2): 142-157. Retrieved from http://comminfolit.org

Souder, L. (2011). The ethics of scholarly peer review: A review of the literature. *Learned Publishing, 24*(1): 55-71. doi: 10.1087/20110109

Swain, B. (2012, September 3). Smart writing: It's good to be published, and better to be understood. *The Weekly Standard, 17*(47). Retrieved from http://www.weeklystandard.com/keyword/Writing

Taylor, M. (2012, January 16). Academic publishers have become enemies of science. *The Guardian*. Retrieved from http://www.guardian.co.uk/science/2012/jan/16/academic-publishers-enemies-science

Taylor & Francis. (2012). College & Undergraduate Libraries—Instructions for authors. Retrieved from http://www.tandfonline.com/action/authorSubmission?journalCode=wcul20&page=instructions

Thomson Reuters. (2011, June 28). JCR 2010 Data are now available. Retrieved from http://community.thomsonreuters.com/t5/Citation-Impact-Center/JCR-2010-data-are-now-available/ba-p/20707

Thomson Reuters. (2007). Emerald selects ScholarOne's Manuscript Central for online peer-review. Retrieved from http://scholarone.com/about/press/s1_pr_021207

University of Chicago. (2010). *Chicago Manual of Style* (6th ed.). Chicago, IL: University of Chicago Press.

Valauskas, E.J. (1997, September). "Waiting for Thomas Kuhn: First Monday and the evolution of electronic journals." *Journal of Electronic Publishing* 3(1). doi: http://dx.doi.org/10.3998/3336451.0003.104

VanScoy, A., & Oakleaf, M. J. (2008). Evidence vs. anecdote: Using syllabi to plan curriculum-integrated information literacy instruction. *College & Research Libraries, 69*(6), 566-575.

Via, B. (1996). Publishing in the journal literature of library and information science: A survey of manuscript review processes and acceptance. *College & Research Libraries, 57*(4): 365-76.

Vix, H., & Buckman, K. (2012). Academic librarians: Status, privileges, and rights. *Journal of Academic Librarianship* 38(1): 20-25.

Weller, A. (2001). *Editorial peer review: Its strengths and weaknesses.* Medford, NJ: American Society for Information Science and Technology.

West J., Bergstrom, T., & Bergstrom C. (2010). Big Macs and Eigenfactor scores: Don't let correlation coefficients fool you. *Journal of the American Society of Information Science and Technology* 61(9): 1800-1807. doi: 10.1002/asi.21374

Xia, J. (2012). Positioning open access journals in a LIS journal ranking. *College & Research Libraries* 73(2): 134-135.

Index